POCKET GUIDE

Miami

Architecture

POCKET GUIDE TO
Miami
Architecture

JUDITH PAINE McBRIEN

Illustrations by John F. DeSalvo

Foreword by Elizabeth Plater-Zyberk

W. W. NORTON & COMPANY

New York • London

The illustrations in this book are dedicated to
Professor Thomas A. Spain, an inspirational teacher and artist.
For historic/location research, we gratefully acknowledge
the help of Carolyn Klepser, Victor Santana, and Ellen Uguccioni.

For information about special discounts for bulk purchases, please contact
W. W. NortonSpecial Sales at specialsales@wwnorton.com or 800-233-4830

Manufacturing by Malloy Printing
Book design by Jonathan Lippincott
Composition: Joe Lops
Production manager: Leeann Graham

Library of Congress Cataloging-in-Publication Data

McBrien, Judith Paine.
 Pocket guide to Miami architecture / Judith Paine McBrien ;
illlustrations by John F. DeSalvo. — 1st ed.
    p. cm.
 Includes index.
 ISBN 978-0-393-73306-8 (pbk.)
 1. Architecture—Florida—Miami Region—Tours.
 2. Miami Region (Fla.)—Buildings, structures, etc.—Tours.
 3. Miami Region (Fla.)—Tours. I. DeSalvo, John F. II. Title.
 NA735.M4M39 2012
 720.9759'381dc23

                              2011025457

ISBN: 978-0-393-73306-8 (pbk.)

W. W. Norton & Company, Inc., 500 Fifth Avenue, New York, N.Y. 10110
www.wwnorton.com
W. W. Norton & Company Ltd., Castle House, 75/76 Wells Street, London W1T 3QT

0 9 8 7 6 5 4 3 2 1

CONTENTS

FOREWORD:
THE IMAGE OF SOUTH FLORIDA

Architecture is not necessarily one's first memory of South Florida. More evocative may be the landscape—the beaches and waterways, the ubiquitous lawns and tree-canopied streets. Yet there is an architectural collection that rewards examination, a history of a region's efforts to attract and impress visitors and residents. "Build it and they will come" applies here.

This book offers the ideal opportunity to become acquainted with South Florida architecture. John de Salvo and Judith Paine McBrien present the region's exemplary buildings with revealing images and text. De Salvo's drawings lift the veil of landscape and urban infrastructure that often conceal or distract attention. McBrien's descriptions provide history and encourage observation of detail, teaching the reader to observe and analyze design and composition.

The collection focuses on Miami, Miami Beach, and Coral Gables, the original urban settlements of South Florida. Evolving in building type and image, from frontier trading post to new communities promising a new life, these cities are now the metropolitan core, an international destination for business and culture.

Native Floridians found the banks of Biscayne Bay and the Miami River an amenable location for living and trading, and so did the late nineteenth-century settlers from the North. Miami's urban beginning was a village with streets and blocks of small houses, and a few larger sites receiving hotels that looked like large houses. A number of the first wood buildings in Florida cracker style can still be found embedded in the subtropical landscape of Coconut Grove. Their younger relative, the bungalow, represents the transition to a masonry city.

In this second period, the community-building idealism of the Progressive Era inspired the founding of Miami Beach and "The City Beautiful" Coral Gables. Both were designed in the manner of the Anglo-American garden city suburb, with town centers and nearby residential neighborhoods. Both cities were originally envisioned in the Mediterranean style, seeking connection with a longer cultural history. Coral Gables hewed to that image, even codifying it, while Miami Beach moved on to a third period of development with Art Deco and Moderne architecture.

And so the region evolved with architectural character specific to

7

place. Miami remains eclectic, reflecting the diversity of its provenance. Coral Gables treasures its Mediterranean character. And Miami Beach encourages innovative additions to its Art Deco history, preserved in a mile-square historic district listed on the National Register of Historic Places.

This book will take you on an enjoyable tour of South Florida's history. With its design heritage as a guide, you will encounter the trajectory of twentieth-century placemaking, a stage set for the contemporary architecture that continues to express the ambitions of its predecessors.

Elizabeth Plater-Zyberk, FAIA
Distinguished Professor and Dean
University of Miami

INTRODUCTION

Miami, Miami Beach, and Coral Gables, all cities that developed in the twentieth century, tell a fascinating story of artifice, innovation, charm, and international influence. The *Pocket Guide to Miami Architecture* offers a sampling of the buildings that help make it so. The book is designed to be easily carried and consulted. It includes 102 original architectural renderings by architect John DeSalvo and individual essays about particularly notable structures, old and new, which were selected as representative of an architect's work, a neighborhood, event, or person. For those who wish to learn more, there are several excellent comprehensive guide options available.

Unlike many cities that evolved as trading or transport hubs, Miami and Miami Beach are sudden, intentional urban constructs. Miami and Miami Beach were invented as tourist destinations; Coral Gables as an ideal City Beautiful. From the very beginning their success depended upon being, and being perceived as, physically attractive. A warm climate was not enough. Although sunny southern Florida was a welcome refuge during winter months, for permanent residents summers before air-conditioning were stifling.

Early on, the cities benefited from new railroad connections and boom times. They grew as acts of speculative will. But what should they look like? In an area full of mangrove thickets and tropical swamps, there was little to suggest building styles that would appeal to those with disposable incomes and leisure time. Nor were there earlier extant Native American or European settlements to inspire. Still, developers were undaunted. The Bay of Biscayne was scenic, the environment could be manipulated, and architectural types could be imported, as indeed they soon were.

The five tours of the *Pocket Guide to Miami Architecture* are a selective journey through time and place: Coral Gables, Miami, and Miami Beach. The first tour includes both the City of Coral Gables and the adjacent historic Miami neighborhood of Coconut Grove, once a separate town. It begins, fittingly, with the Jorge M. Perez Architecture Center at the University of Miami in Coral Gables. The architecture program at the University of Miami has not only educated thousands of students but also encouraged new ideas in planning and architecture that are shaping the community in the 21st century. Coral Gables is a living museum of urban planning and architectural styles, particularly the Mediterranean Revival. The magnificent Biltmore Hotel and Country Club sets the tone: look for red barrel tile roofs, crisp stucco façades, and ornamented doorways. Coconut Grove includes the oldest buildings in the book, vernacular structures such as the Ransom Everglades School "Pagoda" designed with the climate in mind and materials at hand, including insect-resistant Dade County pine and oolitic limestone.

The City of Miami is explored in two tours. The first and longer tour includes the southern section of the city along Biscayne Bay, the Brickell Avenue corridor, and much of the core of downtown Miami. Here you will find modern high-rise residential structures such as the Atlantis, made famous in the opening shots of the television show *Miami Vice*, and the latest skyscrapers as well as civic structures and churches.

The second City of Miami tour continues along Biscayne Bay before heading to the historic enclave of Buena Vista and then west and south to the Overton neighborhood's Lyric Theater and the north bank of the Miami River. Don't miss the Miami Times Building, now known as Freedom Tower, where thousands of Cubans became United States—and Miami—residents, bringing a large Latin presence to the city, or the Bacardi USA building with its striking tile murals.

Just across the Bay of Biscayne is the city of Miami Beach, the glamorous sister of big city Miami. Quaker John Collins from New Jersey planted portions of it as an avocado farm, but it was envisioned as a modest seaside resort by the Lummus Brothers and soon thereafter as a playground for the rich by Carl Fisher, especially on the Biscayne Bay side. By the roaring twenties Miami Beach was in full swing with Spanish Revival mansions and even a sophisticated bohemian enclave called Espanola Way. The first tour focuses upon the area south of 15th Street called South Beach. It was here in the 1930s that a truly American style developed inspired by Art Deco ideas. The tour showcases hotels and other buildings designed by Lawrence Murray Dixon, Henry Hohauser, Albert Anis, and Roy France that are charming, imaginative, and increasingly sophisticated. The second Miami Beach tour takes us north to the iconic Fontainebleau and Eden Roc hotels designed by Morris Lapidus, the legendary Lincoln Road, Frank Gehry's impressive New World Symphony headquarters, and Herzog & deMeuron's innovative parking garage.

Over the past century all three cities have been nourished by diverse cultures. Miami has become a hemispheric financial center, Coral Gables built upon its Spanish Revival identity, and Miami Beach attracts an international crowd. The cities are both international and distinctly American. The *Pocket Guide to Miami Architecture* explores these contrasts and connections. We invite you to begin.

TOUR 1: CORAL GABLES AND COCONUT GROVE

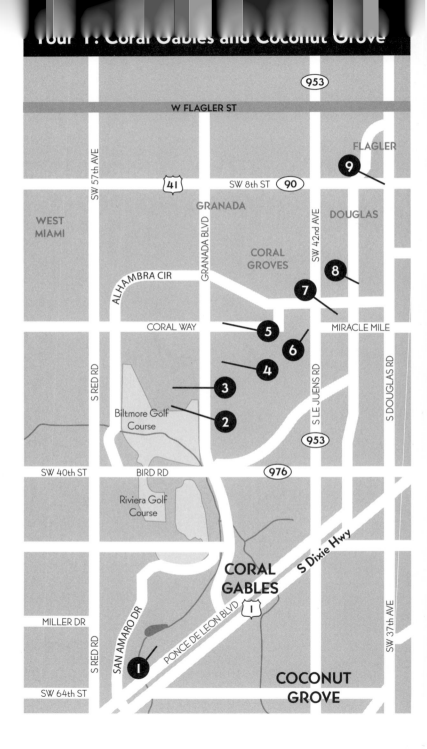

953

W FLAGLER ST

SW 57th AVE

FLAGLER

9

41   SW 8th ST   90

GRANADA

WEST
MIAMI

GRANADA BLVD

SW 42nd AVE

DOUGLAS

CORAL
GROVES

ALHAMBRA CIR

8

7

CORAL WAY

5

MIRACLE MILE

S RED RD

6

4

3

2

Biltmore Golf
Course

S LE JUENS RD

S DOUGLAS RD

953

SW 40th ST   BIRD RD   976

Riviera Golf
Course

S Dixie Hwy

CORAL
GABLES

1

SW 37th AVE

MILLER DR

SAN AMARO DR

1

PONCE DE LEON BLVD

SW 64th ST

S RED RD

COCONUT
GROVE

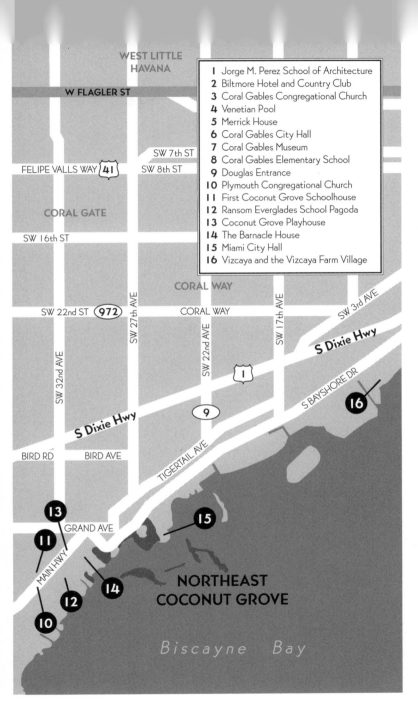

WEST LITTLE HAVANA

W FLAGLER ST

SW 7th ST

FELIPE VALLS WAY **41**

SW 8th ST

CORAL GATE

SW 16th ST

CORAL WAY

SW 22nd ST **972**

CORAL WAY

SW 27th AVE

SW 22nd AVE

SW 17th AVE

SW 3rd AVE

S Dixie Hwy

SW 32nd AVE

1

S Dixie Hwy

9

S BAYSHORE DR

16

BIRD RD

BIRD AVE

TIGERTAIL AVE

13

GRAND AVE

15

11

MAIN HWY

14

12

NORTHEAST
COCONUT GROVE

10

Biscayne Bay

JORGE M. PEREZ SCHOOL OF ARCHITECTURE

University of Miami
Léon Krier with Merrill Pastor Architects and Ferguson Glasgow Schuster Soto, 2004

The University of Miami's Jorge M. Perez Architecture Center seems a perfect fit for an academic edifice: its complexity invites discussion while its functionality serves multiple student and professorial purposes. The 8,200-square-foot Center, home of the School of Architecture, makes a grand statement on this low-scale campus. The structure consists of two connected buildings: the octagonal 144-seat Stanley and Jewell Glasgow Lecture Hall, and the long, narrow Irvin Korach gallery building featuring 150 running feet of exhibition space that includes a small office/conference room core and the 40-seat multimedia Marshall and Vera Lea Rinker classroom. Other components include an arched loggia running the length of the gallery building and a square, flat-roofed porte cochere/pavilion with arches on three sides that marks the main entrance to the Glasgow Lecture Hall. The thick-walled masonry structure, faced with smooth stucco, is as whitewashed as a Santorini villa. Léon Krier (b. 1946), a noted architect and urban planner, is a champion of tradition. In the Perez Architecture Center he uses classical forms, including a pediment, anthemia, and arches, but reinterprets them as simplified shapes to amplify the play of light and shadow. The bell tower (though with no bell) and exterior buttresses likewise reference historical prototypes.

CG-2 BILTMORE HOTEL AND COUNTRY CLUB

1200 Anastasia Avenue
Schultze and Weaver, 1926
Historic name: Miami-Biltmore Hotel
Conference Center addition architect: Barry Berg

The Biltmore Hotel and Country Club was the centerpiece of developer George Merrick's dream to create a beautiful city. Incorporated as a city in 1925 after only four years of existence, Coral Gables had homes but no landmark. The 400-room Biltmore Hotel instantly became so, not only as the tallest building in south Florida but also as the center for activities drawing the rich and famous to Coral Gables. Inspired by the Giralda Bell Tower of the Seville Cathedral in Spain, Schultze and Weaver designed a Y-shaped plan consisting of a 10-story central pavilion with 2 flanking wings. Additional rear wings frame the courtyard, pool and other amenities. Teaming up with Biltmore hotelier John Bowman, Merrick hired architects Leonard Schultze (1877–1951) and S. Fullerton Weaver (1879–1939), who had just finished the Los Angeles Biltmore Hotel, to create a striking structure broadly inspired by Mediterranean architecture. In the next few years they would design other notable area buildings (see M1-13 and M2-4). Note the rich tawny color scheme, the ceiling frescoes, travertine marble and mahogany finishes. The Biltmore has suffered but survived economic downturns, and today, operated by a private consortium but owned by the City of Coral Gables, its future seems secure.

CG-3 CORAL GABLES CONGREGATIONAL CHURCH

3010 De Soto Boulevard
Kiehnel and Elliott, 1925
Additions: 1950, Fellowship Hall; 1952, Sunday school; 1960, Chapel and offices

It shouldn't be surprising that the first public building completed in Coral Gables was a Congregational Church. George Merrick (1886–1942) was the son of Reverend Solomon Merrick—a Congregational minister no less—and dedicated this church to him. The modest-sized church was sited on axis directly south of the grand Biltmore Hotel, on which construction would soon begin. Archival drawings show a long rectangular mirror pool, never executed, connecting the two visually by reflecting their towers. Merrick no doubt hoped that his real estate dreams would be blessed. He chose one of his favorite architects, Richard Kiehnel (1870–1944), to design the concrete and stucco church as a basic rectangle with a center aisle and two side aisles and a bell tower to the south. The fellowship hall and Sunday school areas were added in the 1950s; the Moye Chapel and administrative wings in the 1960s. Kiehnel enlivens the composition at the entrance and bell tower by adding sumptuous swirling ornamentation here made of cast concrete, in a style called Churrigueresque, named after Spanish architect José Benito Churriguera (1665–1725). This element adds a robust yet refined character to the exterior. Note the "swan's neck" pediment, a hallmark of early Coral Gables architecture.

CG-4 VENETIAN POOL

2701 De Soto Boulevard
Denman Fink and Phineas Paist, 1924
Historic name: The Venetian Pool and Casino

In 1923, George Merrick, rather than fill in an existing coral rock quarry that was in the midst of his planned development for Coral Gables, had it transformed into the Venetian Pool, a watery fantasy inspired by both Italian and Spanish design. He enlisted two imaginative designers to carry it out: his uncle, Denman Fink (1881–1956), an accomplished artist who had moved to South Florida in 1914, and architect Phineas Paist (1873–1937), who as Merrick's "Supervising Architect" would shape the future of Coral Gables. During the building of Coral Gables, Fink was appointed art director, and he must have had fun with this project. The result of the two men's work is a somewhat over-the-top but still enchanting stage set replete with waterfalls, a loggia, an arched bridge, an island, and two masonry towers made to look old. The irregular-shaped pool is filled with 820,000 gallons of water and drained daily during the summer. The interior includes decorative painting on ceilings, trusses, and beams as well as an octagonal room with a fountain in the center. The Venetian Pool remains a tourist and local favorite, with a steady variety of programs that attract visitors.

SE

k, 1906

920s, as George Merrick dreamt of planning a beautiful city, nas it that his childhood home provided inspiration for the name "Co. Gables." His father, Reverend Solomon Merrick, bought the Gregory Homestead sight unseen when he moved his family to Florida from Duxbury, Massachusetts, in 1899. By 1906, George's mother, Althea Merrick, had greatly altered and expanded the small cabin originally on the site. She incorporated details of colonial New England architecture familiar to her and added elements appropriate to the tropical climate. Note the sunburst pediment that peeks through the veranda roof, the Palladian window above, sidelights on the double front door, and the broad gabled roof. For shelter from the hot Florida sun, she added a wide porch supported by twenty-two white columns on two sides of the house. The home is built of oolitic limestone, which was quarried nearby from what is now the Venetian Pool (see CG-4), and topped with an orange Ludowicki tile roof. George moved away after marriage, but his mother stayed on until her death in 1937. Subsequent owners preserved Merrick family memorabilia, and the home, restored to its 1920s appearance, is currently administered by the City of Coral Gables as a historic site.

CG-6 CORAL GABLES CITY HALL

405 Biltmore Way
Harold Steward and Phineas Paist, 1928

Architect Phineas Paist drew on his Philadelphia roots when he patterned the Coral Gables City Hall after William Strickland's Philadelphia Merchants' Exchange (1834). Like the Exchange, City Hall sits on a triangular plot facing several streets, most notably Miracle Mile, the gateway thoroughfare to Coral Gables from Miami. City Hall also links the residential area behind it with the commercial area it faces. But the most striking similarity they share is the 3-story curving apse, a semicircular rotunda with a smooth base containing regularly spaced casement windows and a stone balustrade. In the center is the Coral Gables coat of arms designed by Denman Fink. In Philadelphia, the tower above the rotunda is circular, but in Coral Gables, the campanile is a three-stage, nearly square structure that includes a clock tower topped by a bronze belfry. Inside the tower is an impressive gilt and multicolored mural painted by Denman Fink that was restored by John St. John (1911–1986) in 1957. Young women's faces represent the seasons of spring, summer, and fall; winter is an old man. Florida vegetation is depicted on the four sides of the dome.

CG-7 CORAL GABLES MUSEUM

2325 Salzedo Street
Phineas Paist, 1939
East addition, 1954; conversion to office space, 1976
Renovation and addition: Jorge L. Hernandez Architects, 2010
Historic name: Old Police and Fire Station

The City of Coral Gables was an early beneficiary of the federal Works Progress Administration programs that began in 1935 to provide jobs in the Depression. Within two years WPA workers had constructed the Coral Gables Woman's Club and Library, thanks in part to Woman's Club President Mrs. L. L. Langford, who helped secure these government funds. The second WPA project came soon afterward, a new fire station and police building that was one of the last designs of renowned architect Phineas Paist (see CG-4, CG-6). With a 1954 addition to the east, the 2-story L-shaped building, made of masonry faced with keystone coral, includes a three-bay fire station and 4-story tower on Salzedo Street and police offices, a courtroom, and holding cells on Aragon Street. Two large fireman heads sculpted by Theresa Keller mark the fire engine portals while cast-concrete pelicans above the police station entrance symbolize those individuals willing to sacrifice for the community's safety. After the original and later tenants left, structural deterioration followed. Fortunately the building was saved and recently renovated by architect Jorge Hernandez (b. 1956) to become the Coral Gables Museum and Historic Preservation offices. Inspired by classical Greek temples, Hernandez also designed a new 3,000-square-foot addition, the Robert and Marian Fewell Gallery.

CG-8 CORAL GABLES ELEMENTARY SCHOOL

105 Minorca Avenue
Kiehnel and Elliott, 1923–26

George Merrick knew that schools were essential to attract families to his dream city and hired talented architect Richard Kiehnel to design the first one. The Coral Gables Elementary School, built and expanded over three years, was one of the earlier structures completed in Coral Gables. It thus helped define the style, scale, materials, and colors for future development: masonry finished with warm beige stucco; red clay barrel tile roofs; arcades; contrasting decorative block and cast-concrete ornament all wrapped up in a southern Mediterranean package. Kiehnel placed the 2-story school facing south on Minorca Avenue and designed it with an arcaded ground floor supporting a second story of regularly spaced columns and a decorative block balustrade that is protected by a barrel tile roof. Twin towers and paired arches terminate the building on both ends. Within two years the school required more space, so Kiehnel designed the auditorium fronting west on Ponce de Leon Boulevard. With its templelike form that protrudes from the wall and its triple-arcaded entrance supporting an open arcade, many people assume that the 600+-seat auditorium is the main entrance to the school. It's not, but it served for many years as a central meeting place for the entire community.

CG-9 DOUGLAS ENTRANCE

800 Douglas Entrance, SW corner of Douglas Road (SW 37th Street) and the Tamiami Trail (SW 8th Street)
Walter DeGarmo, Denman Fink, Phineas Paist, 1927
Historic name: La Puerta del Sol
Office towers: Spillis Candela & Partners, 1986

Adding to the Mediterranean theme of Coral Gables, Merrick planned walled architectural entrances with arched openings and spacious plazas beyond. Five were built, each designed differently: the Granada Entrance at Granada Boulevard and SW 8th Street, which was based on the Old City Gate in Granada, Spain; the Commercial Entrance, also known as the Alhambra Entrance, at the intersection of Alhambra Circle, Madeira Avenue, and Douglas Road; the Coral Way Entrance at the intersection of Columbus Boulevard and Indian Mound Trail; the Country Club Prado Entrance at Red Road and SW 8th Street, with ornamental pillars; and the Douglas Entrance, the main entrance from Miami and the northernmost gateway into Coral Gables. The main 3-story entrance building has a rusticated base and terminates in a 90-foot belfry. The 40-foot quoined archway, the focus of the composition, has a cartouche instead of a keystone at the center and was intended as a traffic gateway but was closed as part of the 1986 site redevelopment. The room over the archway that connects two buildings originally housed a library, now moved, but the handsome ballroom at the top of a grand staircase in the tower building remains. Walter DeGarmo (1876–1952) was among the chief designers for Coral Gables.

CG-10 PLYMOUTH CONGREGATIONAL CHURCH

3400 Devon Road
J. Clinton MacKenzie, 1917

In 1901 the Plymouth Congregational Church hired Solomon G. Merrick to be its first minister. Later, his son George would not only develop Coral Gables but would also be among the church trustees that selected J. Clinton MacKenzie as the architect for this new church. New York–based MacKenzie (1872–1940) was well connected among the elite for whom he designed estates on Long Island. He was also an accomplished yachtsman, an interest shared with Commodore Ralph Munroe (see CG-14), who had donated property for the first chapel. The Spanish Mission style inspired the church, from its original rectangular plan to the twin bell towers, curvilinear gable roof, and elaborate entrance, including a 375-year-old hand-carved walnut door brought from a monastery in the Pyrenees Mountains. But it is the native oolitic limestone, so-called because the small rounded particles in the stone look like eggs, that is used to construct the building that makes the church so striking. A lone Spanish stonemason named Felix Rebom did all the stonework. In 1954 the church was enlarged by Miami architect Robert Law Weed, who added two transepts and a new chancel. Five years later, additional buildings were added, including a church office building and fellowship hall.

CG-11 FIRST COCONUT GROVE SCHOOLHOUSE

3429 Devon Road
1887

This stark white board-and-batten building exemplifies how a simple structure can represent a complex history. It was first constructed as a Sunday school in 1887 at the urging of Isabella Peacock, who, with her husband, ran the famous Peacock Inn as a gathering place for Coconut Grove's bohemian clientele. As such, the building was the forerunner of the Plymouth Congregational Church (see CG-10). Using salvaged lumber from shipwrecks, the structure is a one-room rectangle topped with a simple bell tower with two shuttered windows on each side and a gable roof covered with wood shingles. Its first preacher was Charles E. Stowe, the son of author and abolitionist Harriet Beecher Stowe. From 1889 to 1894 it was rented as the area's first public schoolhouse until a larger facility opened. This little building was also the first meeting place for the Housekeepers Club, which became the Women's Club of Coconut Grove. For the next sixty-five years it underwent many changes as a private residence, until in 1969 James Ryder, the founder of the Ryder transportation systems corporation, bought the building and had it moved from 2916 Grand Avenue to its present sequestered site on the grounds of the Plymouth Congregation Church.

CG-12 RANSOM EVERGLADES SCHOOL PAGODA

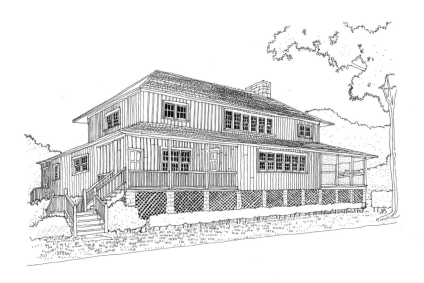

3575 Main Highway
Greene & Wicks, 1902

Buildings with nicknames are often the most beloved, and so it is with the Ransom School "Pagoda." Its double-hipped roof, said to recall Oriental tiered towers, was an exotic reference for the main building of a new school founded by Williams College graduate and Buffalo, New York, attorney Paul C. Ransom (1863–1907) that began as the Pine Knot Camp in 1896. In 1902 this building and a northern campus were added; the school became known then as the Adirondack-Florida School. A fine example of vernacular architecture, the 2-story board-and-batten–sided building is made of termite-resistant and now rare Dade County pine. The 76-by-40-foot structure is anchored by thirty-nine piers of native coral rock, or oolite, a material also used to construct the main chimney. Inside, the main room extends two stories and includes three large fireplaces. On the first floor two verandas, one enclosed and once used as a sleeping porch, face Biscayne Bay. Upstairs rooms are now faculty offices. Architects Edward Brodhead Green (1855–1950; Cornell University, 1878) and William Sydney Wicks (1854–1919; Massachusetts Institute of Technology, 1877) were among the nation's first architecture school graduates; their highly successful firm helped shape Buffalo's future as well as Ransom's innovative school.

CG-13 COCONUT GROVE PLAYHOUSE

3500 Main Highway
Kiehnel and Elliott, 1926
Alfred Browning Parker, 1955

Much has changed since January 1, 1927 when patrons crowded into the 1,500-seat Coconut Grove Theater to see D. W. Griffith's new moving picture, *The Sorrows of Satan*. But the façade of the building remains remarkably intact. Richard Kiehnel, the design partner of Kiehnel and Elliot, placed the 3-story masonry structure on a diagonal facing busy Main Highway and recessed the entire central bay. The entrance is the most elaborate element of the symmetrical scheme: four white concrete spiral columns topped with finials flank a canopied entry with arched cutouts and medallions on the wall above. The effect is subdued elegance. Ground floor storefronts still exist on either side of the doorway; offices were on the second floor; and rental apartments, with Juliet balconies and decorated window treatments, on the third. Nevertheless, some alterations to the original building have occurred. Once painted pink, the Playhouse is now Wedgwood blue, an unusual choice for the area. Originally, the entry culminated in a grand parapet above the roofline, long since removed. In 1955 the Playhouse lost some historic interior ornament when it was converted to a performing arts center. Nevertheless, the building's continued existence reflects its value to the community.

CG-14 THE BARNACLE HOUSE

3485 Main Highway
Ralph Munroe, 1891

Visitors walking down the long path through the tropical hardwood hammock to the Barnacle House enter a world that early Coconut Grove settler Ralph Munroe (1851–1933) saw when he built his home in 1891 on his 40-acre (now 5-acre) property overlooking Key Biscayne. The site, design, and materials of this wood and stucco structure reflect his keen knowledge of the southern Florida climate. Note the 2-story veranda providing shade from the sun while open to ocean breezes; the tall-hipped roof to capture rising hot air; and the flowing interior spaces that maximize natural ventilation. Munroe, known for his yacht designs, exhibits the same superb craftsmanship in the house details. He must have had a sense of humor, too, naming his house "the barnacle" after the octagonal living room. Originally a single story, Monroe added a second story in 1908 and a library wing on the northeast side later. The property also includes a boathouse and a reconstructed pioneer cabin. Monroe was an avid photographer, naturalist, and community leader. Fortunately for us, the entire property stayed in the Monroe family until 1972, so historic artifacts remained largely intact. In 1973, the State of Florida purchased the Barnacle as a historic site and opened it to the public.

CG-15 MIAMI CITY HALL

3500 Pan American Drive
Fred J. Gelhaus & B. W. Resser and Delano & Aldrich, 1930–38
Renovation: R. J. Heisenbottle Architects, 2001

Unlike most city halls, the Miami City Hall is not located downtown but rather 5 miles south. It began as a Pan-American Airlines passenger terminal on Dinner Key in Biscayne Bay. The passenger terminal, airplane hangers, and other facilities served as the base for Pan Am's inter-American clipper ship operations to South and Central America. After Pan Am's final flight in August 1945, the City of Miami purchased 39 acres of the Dinner Key property and in 1954 adapted the 2-story white rectangular terminal as City Hall. Note the colorful frieze of globes and risings suns connected at the corners by sculptured eagles just underneath the cornice line. Wings on either side of the lobby create additional space. While the building's exterior is plain, the lobby includes a ceiling decorated with signs of the zodiac and once contained a huge 3.5-ton revolving world globe, now at the Miami Science Museum. The restored wall murals depict the history of flight from Leonardo da Vinci's designs to the famous Pan Am clipper planes. Fred J. Gelhaus, an airport engineer for the Caribbean system of Pan American Airlines, is credited with the basic design, but noted New York firm Delano & Aldrich developed the full plans.

3251 South Miami Avenue
F. Burrall Hoffman; Diego Suarez, landscape architect; Paul Chalfin, interiors,
1913-16; gardens, 1914-1920s
Restoration and glass roof over courtyard: David Wolfberg, 1978-89

Vizcaya, the winter home of International Harvester Company heir James Deering (1859-1925), is among America's grandest estates. Viewed from Biscayne Bay, the white building, reportedly based on the eighteenth-century Villa Rezzonico in the Italian Veneto, is a simple but imposing central mass flanked by twin towers. Inside are 70 rooms situated around a hollow core plan and decorated with art, furniture, and artifacts mainly from sixteenth- to nineteenth-century European sources. The 50-acre property (once 180 acres) still includes the original farm complex and formal gardens based on Renaissance and French designs. That this eclectic estate seems nonetheless harmonious is all the more remarkable because it results from the collaboration of three designers who knew little of each other and seemed to care less. Deering's maestro was painter Paul Chalfin (1874-1959), a well-connected aesthete hired to oversee the interior. Only in 1912, after Chalfin had purchased entire rooms of furnishings, was architect Francis Burrall Hoffman (1882-1980) hired to design a building envelope. Finally, in 1914 young Colombian Diego Suarez (1888-1974), who had just completed landscape studies in Italy, was brought aboard to design the extensive gardens, but left only two years later. Don't miss the barge breakwater with sculptures by A. Stirling Calder.

TOUR 2: MIAMI 1

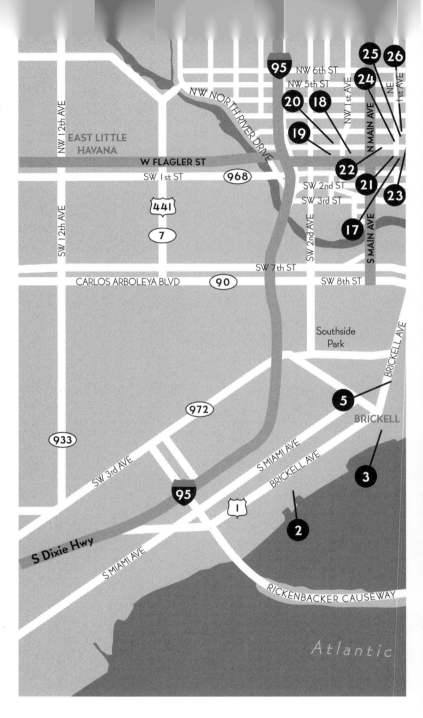

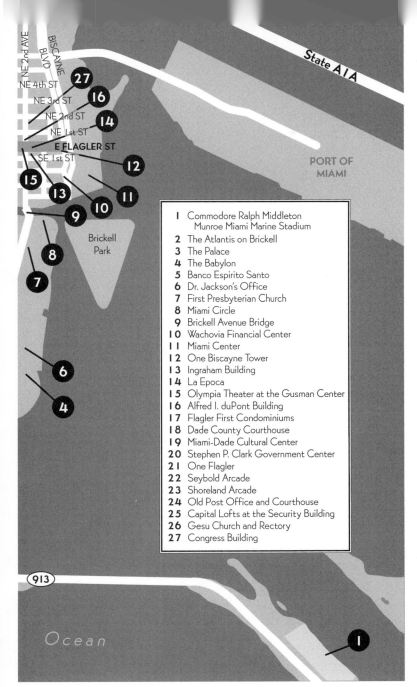

NE 2nd AVE
BISCAYNE BLVD
NE 4th ST
NE 3rd ST
NE 2nd ST
NE 1st ST
E FLAGLER ST
SE 1st ST

State A1A

PORT OF MIAMI

Brickell Park

1   Commodore Ralph Middleton
    Munroe Miami Marine Stadium
2   The Atlantis on Brickell
3   The Palace
4   The Babylon
5   Banco Espirito Santo
6   Dr. Jackson's Office
7   First Presbyterian Church
8   Miami Circle
9   Brickell Avenue Bridge
10 Wachovia Financial Center
11 Miami Center
12 One Biscayne Tower
13 Ingraham Building
14 La Epoca
15 Olympia Theater at the Gusman Center
16 Alfred I. duPont Building
17 Flagler First Condominiums
18 Dade County Courthouse
19 Miami-Dade Cultural Center
20 Stephen P. Clark Government Center
21 One Flagler
22 Seybold Arcade
23 Shoreland Arcade
24 Old Post Office and Courthouse
25 Capital Lofts at the Security Building
26 Gesu Church and Rectory
27 Congress Building

913

Ocean

MI-1 COMMODORE RALPH MIDDLETON MUNROE MIAMI MARINE STADIUM

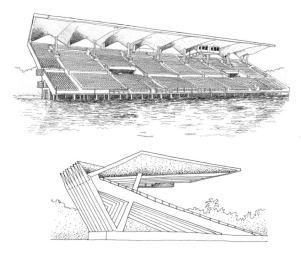

3501 Rickenbacker Causeway
Architect: Pancoast, Ferendino, Skeels, Grafton and Burnham
Engineer: Digmun Engineers, 1963

Cuban-born Hilario Candela (b. 1938) was just a youngster at Pancoast, Ferendino, Skeels, Grafton and Burnham when the city of Miami chose the firm to design a marine stadium for spectator water sports in the early 1960s. Yet he designed a modern masterpiece. Inspired by Latin American architects who were exploring concrete as an expressive form maker, including Max Borges in Havana, for whom he briefly worked, Candela understood the dramatic possibilities of poured-in-place concrete. Working with engineer Jack Meyer, he created a 6,566-seat open-air stadium sheltered by a 64-foot cantilevered folded plate roof that is only 6 inches thick. The roof consists of a series of hyperbolic paraboloids, a twisting shape that follows a convex curve about one axis and a concave curve about the other—a type favored for spanning large areas because its lightweight form requires fewer columnar supports and its curvature discourages water retention. Here, only eight slanting piers support the long roof, while diagonal members provide additional stability on the back. The stadium's waterfront setting overlooking downtown Miami is equally spectacular. Unfortunately, despite no evidence of serious damage, the city closed the stadium after Hurricane Andrew in 1992. New funding promised for renovation offers preservationists hope.

2025 Brickell Avenue
Arquitectonica, 1982

The Atlantis on Brickell is clever, colorful, and bold. It not only put the young firm of Arquitectonica on the international map but also helped rebrand the city of Miami itself: every week the Atlantis was featured in the opening credits of the hit television show *Miami Vice*, symbolizing Miami as a cool, hip place. The façade can be understood as signage. First is the striking 37-foot rectangular hole cut out of the middle of the 20-story glass and steel façade that jolts our visual expectations and arrests our attention. Paradoxically, this void is meant to be seen: the walls are painted a vivid yellow, a red staircase spirals through the space, and a gigantic palm tree seems planted in the air. Next, the use of bold colors continues with the placement of a large red triangle on the east side of the roof balanced by four yellow triangular awnings on the lower floors and by four red columns supporting the entrance canopy. The north façade has a colossal blue grid overlaying the surface, equally emphasizing the horizontal and vertical elements that comprise the plan. Completing this graphic composition of primary colors and shapes is a full-height glass curve facing Biscayne Bay.

1541 Brickell Avenue
Arquitectonica, 1982

In less than four years, the work of Arquitectonica transformed Brickell Avenue into a showplace for cutting-edge design with four signature high-rise residential buildings: the Atlantis (see M1-2), the Imperial (1982), the Villa Regina (1983), and the project that started it all, the Palace. In the late 1970s, billionaire New York real estate entrepreneur Harry Helmsley and his wife, Leona, known for the high-profile Helmsley Palace in Manhattan, sought a Miami presence that bespoke luxury, class, and front-page style. At the same time, changes in Brickell Avenue zoning from single- to multifamily residential offered extraordinary opportunities for dense development, especially for east-side land parcels that extended to the waterfront. Given this chance, Arquitectonica delivered. Taking a cue from the just-completed Babylon (see M1-4), the 252-unit Palace, sometimes referred to as the Palace on Brickell or the Helmsley Palace, continues the ziggurat theme and red color with giant steps that rise 16 stories from the waterfront to intersect and pass through the gridded 42-story building facing Biscayne Bay. On the other side, the ziggurat becomes a vertical "monumental porte cochere," according to the architects. Low-rise townhouses along the waterfront, a 2-level parking garage, and amenities galore complete the complex.

240 SE 14th Street
Arquitectonica, 1979

The Babylon apartment project brought the first wave of public acclaim to the young firm of Arquitectonica. The name recalls the large, legendary city famous in the ancient world for its art and architecture. Major Babylonian monuments were shaped as ziggurats in which each building level "steps up" to a smaller one above. Here, Arquitectonica uses this shape, painted red, as a form to draw attention and add dimension to a short narrow structure built on a site that is almost but not quite directly on the Biscayne Bay waterfront. From a practical standpoint, the shape also met zoning envelope requirements. The 6-story slab is one long terraced residential structure with parking underneath that was conceived as two sections separated by a courtyard. The front ziggurat is a short L, the south side set back from the street as a geometric curtain for the apartment terraces. The west end of the building repeats the color and shape of the frontal ziggurat but acts more fully as a screen for the units behind. White stair and terrace railings emphasize horizontality while offering color contrast. The Babylon is a clever exercise; in terms of form and functionality, Arquitectonica would soon do better (see M1-2).

1395 Brickell Avenue
Kohn Pedersen Fox Associates with SB Architects and Swanke Hayden Connell, 2004

Architect William C. Louie's elegant green-glass design mixes the symbolic and the practical in a 36-story, 1.2-million-square-foot mixed-use building that has already become a Miami favorite. Each use in this post-tensioned concrete structure required different floor plans and column spacing. Offices, accessed from a 4-story atrium on the second floor, occupy floors 2 through 25. Above them, an 11-story atrium sky lobby separates the hotel rooms from the residential condominiums. An adjacent 12-story parking garage completes the program. The building's most striking feature is a 30-story-high concave parabolic arch that is indented in the building's west façade facing the city. The form suggests Miami as a gateway to Latin America, just as Eero Saarinen's Gateway Arch references St. Louis as a gateway to the West. The east side of the structure faces Key Biscayne, so maximizing views for hotel guests and condominium owners required a different geometry. Another theme relates to Miami's connection to the water. For example, to enter the building from Brickell Avenue, pedestrians must pass over a curved pond that lies at the base of the building while the main vehicular drive for the hotel and residences entrances goes underneath a glass-bottomed reflecting pool.

DR. JACKSON'S OFFICE

190 SE 12th Terrace
Architect unknown, 1905

Dr. James M. Jackson (1866–1924), born in White Sulphur Springs, Florida, came to Miami when he was thirty years old as a surgeon for Henry Flagler's railroad. As a civic leader, he was the founding president of the Rotary Club and so beloved a physician that upon his death the Miami City Hospital was renamed in his honor (see M2-12). His home and next-door office-clinic originally stood on NE 2nd Avenue, just north of Flagler Street. Both structures were moved by barge to this site in 1917, but in 2001 his home was demolished. In 1977 the nonprofit Dade Heritage Trust restored his 1-story office/clinic and made the building its headquarters. Since then the little office has had few alterations. It still has its original windows and floors of Dade County pine, much of its hexagonal tilework, and some of Dr. Jackson's furnishings. A long open porch supported by columns faces Biscayne Bay on the east, with the main front porch facing north. A handicapped ramp was added for accessibility. The newly replaced roof replicates the original red Ludowici terra-cotta tile, adding color to the simple white structure that today is nearly hidden by the immense towers that surround it.

609 Brickell Avenue
Lester W. Geisler, 1949

The First Presbyterian Church was first organized in 1896, making it Miami's oldest congregation. Miami developer Henry Flagler donated land to it for the construction of a church, as he did for several other congregations. But Flagler, a Presbyterian himself, went a step further here, funding the construction of the church itself at the corner of East Flagler and SE 3rd Avenue in 1900. In 1947 the congregation left downtown and purchased a 3-acre site on fashionable Brickell Avenue for a new church. Designed in a Mediterranean Revival style by Presbyterian elder and architect Lester Geisler (1900–1996) the 4-story church is entered through three limestone arches above which are three windows and the central gable. On the north side a wing named the Flagler Memorial replicates the exterior of the original 1900 church. The 2-story wing on the south is a simple rectangle with sets of four windows on each level. The stucco and steel church, first painted white, is now distinguished by its bright salmon pink color selected in 1996 to coordinate with the church's centennial celebration materials. Today, Brickell Avenue remains famous, but now as the center for hemispheric financial firm offices and luxury high-rise condominiums that dwarf the handsome church.

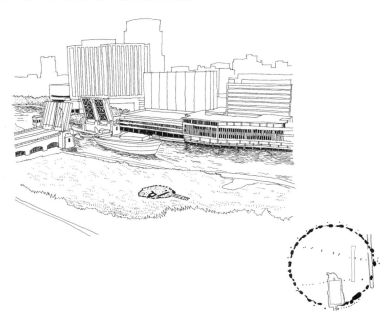

Southern bank of the Miami River near Brickell Avenue and SE 4th Street
2.2 acres

Often touted as America's youngest major metropolis, Miami may in fact be one of the oldest. In 1998 a routine check for historic artifacts required for a new property development at the mouth of the Miami River uncovered an astonishing find when apartment buildings on the proposed project site were demolished: 24 rectangular holes dug into the oolitic limestone bedrock that formed a perfect 38-foot-wide circle. Hundreds of other postholes were found as well. Nothing so complete had been found before. Archaeologists speculate that the footprint represents a ceremonial center built by native Tequesta Indians. The site also yielded an extraordinary cache of other material including ceramics, sacrificial animal skeletons, and shell tools. Radiocarbon dating indicates a settlement circa 100 A.D. and possibly older. Indeed, the Miami Circle appears to be the only preserved cut-in-rock prehistoric structural footprint in the eastern United States. After a lively debate, the State of Florida purchased the site from the private developer and leased it to HistoryMiami to help create a park with interpretive displays and educational programs. Now designated a National Historic Landmark, if plans proceed as expected, soon this ancient, intact Native American site can be accessed in the very heart of modern Miami.

Brickell Avenue at the Miami River
Design: Jorge L. Hernandez, Rafael Portuondo and Mike Sardinas, 1993
Engineer: Kunde, Sprecher & Associates; Portuondo Perotti Architects, 1995

The Brickell Avenue Bridge spanning the Miami River is significant for its engineering, design, and civic presence. The trunnion bascule bridge, which replaced an earlier 1929 structure, is an engineering tour de force, capable of carrying three lanes of traffic in each direction across its 100-foot width and opening in less than a minute. Its twin double leaves divide, and rotate like a seesaw (bascule) around a pivot point (trunnion) on roller bearings before returning to their fixed positions. The span also connects the two most famous thoroughfares in the city, Biscayne Boulevard and Brickell Avenue and thus became a fitting site with which to commemorate the centennial of the Miami's founding in 1896. Specially commissioned artwork was created, the most visible of which is the 37-foot obelisk topped with a Tequesta Indian family designed by renowned Cuban sculptor Manuel Carbonell (b. 1918). It stands on the southeast side of the Brickell Bridge as a kind of Miamian Trajan's Column honoring not an emperor but a Native American tribe whose prehistoric settlement remains, the Miami Circle (see M1-8), are visible below. Other artwork includes bronze bas-reliefs of Florida pioneers William and Mary Brickell, Julia Tuttle, Henry Flagler, D. A. Dorsey, and Marjorie Stoneman Douglas.

WACHOVIA FINANCIAL CENTER

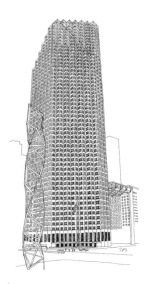

200 South Biscayne Boulevard
Skidmore, Owings & Merrill; associate architect, Spillis Candela & Partners, 1984
Formerly known as the Southeast Financial Center, First Union Financial Center

For more than a quarter of a century, the Wachovia Financial Center, built originally for Southeast Bank, has set a standard for elegant skyscraper design on Biscayne Boulevard. The 2-acre complex consists of a 765-foot-tall, 55-story office tower and a 15-story parking annex. An enclosed walkway that leads to the second-floor banking hall/lobby connects the two structures. Below is an open courtyard landscaped with royal palms. Note how the space frame canopy above the courtyard references Isamu Noguchi's (1904–1988) vertical sculpture, the Challenger Memorial, across the street in Bayfront Park. When built, the structure was the tallest office building in Miami, and it has since become the city's first office building to receive a LEED (Leadership in Energy and Environmental Design) Gold Certification from the U.S. Green Building Council. Its indented zigzag window pattern is a photographer's dream. Seen from certain angles the building appears to form a triangle with a rectangular office tower peeking behind it. The Art Deco–like setbacks that help create this illusion begin above the 43rd floor. This 1.2-million-square-foot complex was among the largest, last, and most successful projects designed by Edward Charles Bassett (1922–1999) of the Skidmore, Owings & Merrill San Francisco office.

201 South Biscayne Boulevard
Pietro Belluschi Architects, 1980–83

Miami Center might have the best location in Miami. It was built on an 8.4 acre site once owned by Henry Flagler himself at the mouth of the Miami River, with Biscayne Bay to the east and Bayfront Park on the north. Two buildings comprise the development: a 35-story hotel on the waterfront that is shifted off axis and a 34-story office tower on Biscayne Boulevard. Both buildings are sheathed in travertine marble and connected by a parking garage and shared meeting spaces. They are also linked by their similar fenestration and nearly identical height. Architect Pietro Belluschi designed a different form for each structure in order to highlight their distinctive uses. The hotel is an equilateral triangle of 8-bay façades with a full-height deep concave curve in between the sides. This shape maximizes views for hotel guests. The office high-rise is a rectangular 10-bay by 7-bay tower with a flat roof. The base is raised on a plinth above street level, and near the top a band of horizontal windows marks the transition to the roof. Belluschi (1899–1994) designed more than 1,000 buildings during his long career and received the American Institute of Architects Gold Medal in 1972.

MI-12 ONE BISCAYNE TOWER

2 South Biscayne Boulevard
Humberto Alonso, Pelayo G. Fraga & Associates, E. H. Gutierrez & Associates, 1974

Every building has a story, but few have as dramatic a tale as One Biscayne Tower. It began in the early 1970s with the availability of this prime site at the corner of Flagler Street, the east-west thoroughfare that divides north from south in Miami, and Biscayne Boulevard. On it would be built the tallest skyscraper in Miami, a 39-story, 620,000-square-foot concrete and glass office tower with nine floors of parking and a planned rooftop private heliport. The building was designed, constructed, and financed by a team of Cuban exiles led by E. H. Gutierrez (b. 1931). Its height, location, and expressive prestressed concrete façade created a stunning modern landmark that redefined Miami's skyline. Note how the horizontal parking floors contrast with the vertical piers and dramatic 6-foot-high windows of the office tower. Its open floor plates, made possible by minimal wall-bearing columns, were planned to appeal to corporate tenants, as was the marble lobby. Unfortunately the high-profile building opened in the midst of an economic recession and it struggled to attract tenants. Yet just a few years later when the markets recovered, the building sold at a record price, a recognition of its superb location and distinctive design.

M1-13 INGRAHAM BUILDING

25 SE 2nd Avenue
Schultze and Weaver, 1927
Renovation: Rodriguez, Khuly, Quiroga, Architects 1990

The 13-story, 200,000-square-foot Ingraham Building is a fitting tribute to its namesake, engineer James E. Ingraham: handsome, efficient, and richly attired. The U-shaped cube rises from the corner of SE 2nd Avenue and SE 1st Street as a Bedford limestone block divided by cornices and belt courses into three main horizontal sections: a base, a midsection with regular-spaced fenestration, and a penthouse level above the 11th floor with arched bifora windows. A truncated hip roof covered with Spanish tiles supported by a bracketed cornice tops the composition. But it is the lobby's scale, colorful vaulted ceilings, and colossal limestone Doric columns that give the Ingraham Building its cachet. Ingraham first visited Florida in 1874 to see his grandfather, then rector of Trinity Episcopal Church in St. Augustine. After working for railroad entrepreneur Henry Plant, he joined Henry Flagler's Florida East Coast Railway Company, rising to become vice president as well as president of Flagler's real estate firm, the Model Land Company. When Ingraham died in 1924, Miami was booming. Construction of a Class A office building in his honor made sense, especially since noted architectural firm Schultze and Weaver was available, with several other projects underway nearby (see CG-2, M2-4).

MI-14 LA EPOCA

200 East Flagler Street
Zimmerman, Saxe and MacBride; E. A. Ehrmann, associate architect 1936
Historic name, Walgreen Drugstore

La Epoca Department Store, where fashionistas now flock, began as a Walgreen's drugstore, part of the company's expansion into Florida that began with a 4,000-square-foot-store in Tampa in 1934. Two years later Walgreen's opened in Miami with this 5-story, 50,000-square-foot streamlined building that curves around the corner with alternating continuous bands of ribbon windows and smooth solid brick. For added visual prominence, the entrance bay extends slightly from the wall plane from the ground floor to the top of the building. The name of the building is placed just above the three paired entry doors. Walgreen's even featured an 88-foot soda fountain counter and a separate ice-cream plant. The structure's simple mass but sure design is by Zimmerman, Saxe and MacBride, Chicago-based Walgreen's firm of choice. Were they perhaps influenced by another famous building with a curved entrance in their own hometown, Louis Sullivan's Carson Pirie Scott Department Store? Before purchasing this building, La Epoca had rented space in the Alfred I. duPont Building (see MI-16) for more than twenty years. With a building with which it could extend its brand name, sales improved and today La Epoca is a fixture on Flagler Street.

OLYMPIA THEATER AT THE GUSMAN CENTER

174 East Flagler Street
John Eberson, 1926
Theater renovation: Morris Lapidus, 1972
Renovations: R. J. Heisenbottle Architects, 1989–96
Renovation of offices to residential: Victor Morales, 1995

From the little ticket booth on the sidewalk with the two-toned columns to the elaborate interior, the Olympia Theater is a fine example of 1920s American theater design. It was developed for Paramount Enterprises Inc. by the man many consider the best in the business, John Eberson (1875–1954). Eberson already had a reputation for transforming dark theaters into "atmospheric" painted stage sets replete with twinkling stars, clouds, castles, gardens, peacocks, and imaginative decorative details. Customers were thus primed for illusion before performances even began. The 1,600-seat Olympia was developed as a wing of a 10-story buff-colored brick and steel office building at the corner of SE 2nd Avenue and East Flagler Street that is 5 bays wide on the east and 9 bays wide on the north. The north façade is unadorned except for the tenth floor, which features a terra-cotta double Flemish scroll pediment with a coat of arms in the center. The theater showcased vaudeville acts from 1929–1954; in 1972, Morris Lapidus oversaw an extensive renovation. In order to ensure its preservation, philanthropist Maurice Gusman purchased the building; he donated it to the City of Miami in 1975. Richard J. Heisenbottle Architects is responsible for more recent work.

ALFRED I. DUPONT BUILDING

169 East Flagler Street
Marsh and Saxelbye, 1939

Few downtown skyscrapers were built in Miami after the 1926 hurricane or during the Great Depression of the 1930s, so the construction of the 17-story Alfred I. duPont Building in 1937 signaled renewed faith in the future of the "Magic City." Built as the headquarters of the Florida National Bank, which Alfred I. duPont (1864-1935) had organized in 1931, the duPont Building is also the only Art Deco/Depression Moderne high-rise in downtown Miami. The black granite banding of the first-floor retail, the sleek stone façade, the setbacks facing NE 2nd Avenue, and the ornate stylized interior details are hallmarks of this architectural style. Note especially the palm trees on the brass elevators, the ceiling of the second-floor banking room with wooden cedar beams painted with motifs derived from Seminole Indian designs, and the ornate teller grillwork. DuPont left Delaware for Jacksonville, Florida, in 1926 and began a second success-ful investment career. William Mulford Marsh (1889-1946) and Harold Frederick Saxelbye (1885-1964) led the most prolific architecture firm in Jacksonville and had already designed duPont's 25-room Epping Forest Mansion on the St. Johns River. When the time came to choose architects to design a skyscraper honoring Alfred I. duPont, they were the obvious choice.

MI-17 FLAGLER FIRST CONDOMINIUMS

101 East Flagler Street
Mowbray & Uffinger, 1922; North tower: H. H. Mundy, 1926
Residential rehabilitation: Roberto M. Martinez Architect, 2005
Historic name: First National Bank of Miami

"Steel Frame Structure Is One of the Most Complete and Up-to-Date in the Entire South," read the *Miami Herald* headline on November 14, 1922, when the First National Bank Building opened at the corner of East Flagler and First Avenue. The 10-story brick and terra-cotta structure was impressive. Its 3-story base is made of Indiana limestone with Corinthian capped pilasters marking each bay, and its interior was finished with marble floors, bronze hardware, hallways of terrazzo, and, for the president's office, mahogany wainscoting. The upper floors follow a regular grid pattern reflecting the building's steel skeletal frame. Note the grand 3-story arched entrance on East Flagler Street flanked by horizontal stonework reminiscent of Italian Renaissance palazzos. The prosperous bank was designed by one of the most prolific and prestigious firms of the day, New York–based Mowbray & Uffinger, which specialized in large-scale commercial structures, especially banks. Several of its buildings are listed on the National Register of Historic Places. In Florida the firm had already completed the Florida National Bank in Jacksonville, the First National Bank in Pensacola, and the First National Bank at Sanford. Senior partner Louis Montayne Mowbray died in 1921, but the firm continued and later reorganized as Uffinger, Foster & Bookwalter.

DADE COUNTY COURTHOUSE

73 West Flagler Street
A. Ten Eyck Brown and August Geiger, 1925
Restoration of Courtroom 6-1: M. C. Harry & Associates, 2006

For decades the 27-story Miami-Dade County Courthouse dominated Miami's skyline. And no wonder: its height, symmetry, setbacks, and roofline made it visibly iconic from every angle. Like the Los Angeles City Hall and Nebraska's State Capitol, the Courthouse also expressed a new way of thinking about what a major civic structure should look like. From now on skyscrapers, not just domed and columned buildings, could signify public use. The courthouse occupies a full city block and rises from a double square base. The first three stories are faced with Stone Mountain granite and decorated with six colossal fluted Doric columns flanked by two pilasters. Above them is an entablature and attic story. The second 3 stories are set back and include six double-story pilasters with Egyptian capitals surmounted by a balustrade. The 7th to the 20th floors form a tower. The slab then changes to an octagonal shape and a further setback occurs at the 24th floor. Topping the courthouse is a 3-story pyramidal roof. Originally the building housed not only courtrooms but also City Hall, county and city jails, and attendant governmental offices. City Hall moved out in 1954 (see CG-15), but the courtrooms remain. Note especially Courtroom 6-1, recently restored.

MIAMI-DADE
CULTURAL CENTER

101 West Flagler Street
Johnson/Burgee, 1984

Where is it again? Although located on Flagler Street in the midst of down-town, finding the Miami-Dade Cultural Center can be daunting. The main entrance is via a single staircase that is set in between high windowless masonry walls that line the sidewalk. Steep stairs lead up to a terrace that is barely visible from the street. Isolated and forbidding, the Miami-Dade Cultural Center manages to be cold in a tropical climate. On the plaza level, three cultural buildings share the space: the Miami-Dade Public Library on the west side, the Historical Museum of Southern Florida, renamed HistoryMiami, on the north side, and the Miami Art Museum, soon to move to a new facility (see M2-6) on the southeast. All share the simple rectan-gular massing, arched openings, pale color, and terra-cotta tile roofs found in California Mission–style architecture. Each, however, has a mannerist twist. The Miami Art Museum seems pushed up against the wall, the Histo-ryMiami building has tiny doorways out of scale with its size, and even the Miami-Dade Public Library, the best of the bunch, has attic windows that seem like afterthoughts. And the plaza itself? With attractive patterned paving but little shade, it's mostly empty.

MI-20 STEPHEN P. CLARK GOVERNMENT CENTER

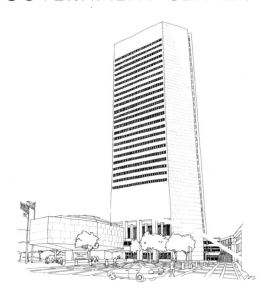

111 Northwest 1st Street
The Stubbins Associates, Inc., 1985

The 30-story Stephen P. Clark Government Center looms large and bland as part of the government campus on Miami's west side. Yet the limestone building, which houses the Miami-Dade County offices, has functioned well by meeting a variety of complex security, programmatic, and circulation requirements, including a second-floor Metro Station that services both the Metrorail and Metromover systems connected by an attractive 2-story glass atrium. The Clark Center, named for a former Miami mayor, was designed at a transition point in the firm of Hugh Stubbins and Associates. In 1983, Stubbins (1912–2006) retired as an active member of the firm, but the office, with new leadership, continued under the name The Stubbins Associates, Inc. The firm's penchant for exterior horizontal window banding can be seen in earlier more distinguished designs, including the Boston Federal Reserve Bank Building, nicknamed "the washboard" (1976), Manhattan's Citicorp Center (1977), and One Cleveland Center (1983). Stubbins, a dedicated Modernist, had a storied career, becoming a protégé of Walter Gropius, the German Bauhaus architect who led the Harvard Graduate School of Design. Stubbins would later direct the school himself before leaving to focus on his thriving architecture practice, where he mentored other designers, including a young I. M. Pei.

14 NE 1st Avenue
Morris Lapidus & Associates, 1952,
Also known as the Foremost Building

At first glance, the plain 15-story gridded glass box facing 1st Avenue seems completely unrelated to the glitzy seductive curves (see MB2-5) associated with architect Morris Lapidus (1902–2001). Indeed, although reportedly the first skyscraper constructed in downtown Miami after World War II, the building is sometimes ignored in the roster of key Lapidus buildings. Nevertheless, the 141,000-square-foot building, first called the Ainsley, then the Foremost, shows a distinctive flair. Most notably, concrete cantilevers mark each floor above the second story on the south façade and wrap around the NE 1st Street corner. The cantilevers create shade and visual interest on what is today a commonplace exterior. In the early 1950s, however, this glazed curtain-wall structure, completed the same year as SOM's iconic Lever House in Manhattan, must have seemed startlingly modern among its neighbors, including the solid red brick across the street (see M1-17). Once dismissed as too kitschy by the architectural establishment, Lapidus's work is being reassessed today. He designed over a thousand buildings, including offices, stores, residences, and a plan for the Lincoln Road Mall (see MB2-16) in Miami Beach. As he titled his autobiography, Too Much Is Never Enough.

M1-22 SEYBOLD ARCADE

36 NE 1st Street
Kiehnel and Elliott, 1921-25
Flagler Street Arcade entrance: Robert Law Weed, 1939

German pioneer John Seybold (1872-1940) was among Miami's most energetic entrepreneurs. He first ran a restaurant, then a famous bakery, developed an exclusive residential neighborhood, now the Spring Garden Historic District, widened part of Wagner Creek to became a canal he named after himself, and hired one of South Florida's leading architectural firms, Kiehnel and Elliott, to build the 2-story Seybold Arcade in 1921 with a grand entrance on 1st Street. As business boomed, he asked the architects, who were completing the Scottish Rite Temple (see M2-14), to add an additional 8 stories. The exterior consists of a horizontal band of ten windows regularly spaced between rounded pilasters and grouped within six vertical piers that rise the full length of the structure. This pattern is repeated across the entire façade. A decorative band of icicle-shaped terra-cotta forms mark the third story. Architect Robert Law Weed (1897-1961) added the 3-story Flagler Street entrance in 1939. At first the new addition housed professional offices, but for the past forty years it has become a leading center for the jewelry trade. Arcades were a popular retail shopping form (see M1-23) when enough property could be assembled to create a through-street corridor in dense downtowns.

120–136 NE 1st Street
Pfeiffer and O'Reilly, 1925
Flagler Street façade renovation: Robert Law Weed, 1939

The 2-story Shoreland Arcade was clearly designed for curb appeal. Its crisp masonry façade is divided into 8 storefront bays with generous windowed arches to invite customers inside. Pilasters dividing the bays add further detail as do the colorful medallions symbolizing events in Florida's history. The interior lobby is more elaborate. The ceiling is coffered, the tile floors are set within terrazzo, and the walls are rusticated masonry. Moreover, care is taken to repeat the scale and style of the exterior arched display windows on the 5 bays leading to the elevator core. Could it be that there is more to this story than shopping? Indeed, the Shoreland Company, known for developing Miami Shores, the Venetian Causeway, and Biscayne Boulevard, originally planned the building not as a stand-alone arcade but as the retail base of its planned 20-story headquarters. The sudden collapse of the real estate market in 1926 abruptly ended that scheme. The next year, the Shoreland Company went bankrupt. But the arcade, which once extended to Flagler Street as well as to NE 1st Avenue, was already finished and has remained nearly intact through the years. Today it is among the last surviving examples of its kind in Miami (see M1-22).

OLD U.S. POST OFFICE AND COURTHOUSE

100 NE 1st Avenue
Oscar Wenderoth, 1914: addition, Kiehnel and Elliott, plans, 1937
Renovation: Architectural Design Consultants, 2002

The old limestone United States Post Office and Courthouse is a prime example of the neoclassical style, the dominant aesthetic for public buildings in America a century ago, especially in self-conscious cities that aspired to be beautiful. The harmonious proportions of the 3-story façade, the quality of materials, and the numerous exquisite details give this simple form a dignity worthy of Miami's first federal building. Note the underside of the tiled hipped roof revealing the wooden brackets once brilliantly polychromed, the layered entablature atop the pilasters, and the repeating dentil, and egg and dart, patterns that add richness to the simple connection between vertical and horizontal planes. Oscar Wenderoth (1871–1938) executed these classical elements with confidence. Wenderoth, named supervising architect for the U.S. Treasury Department in 1912, had previously worked for the federal government before joining the distinguished New York firm of Carrère & Hastings, designers of the New York Public Library. But three years after the appointment to his prestigious post, he suddenly resigned; by 1920 he was completely blind. In 1937 the loggia was enclosed when the building was converted to a bank. In 1948, Kiehnel and Elliott's 1937 plans were followed, adding 2-story wings to the east and south elevations.

M1-25 CAPITOL LOFTS AT THE SECURITY BUILDING

117 NE 1st Avenue
Robert Greenfield, 1926
Residential rehabilitation: Rodriguez & Quiroga Architects, 2006

Built for the Dade County Security Company, which was among the most important financial institutions in Florida, this 16-story granite, brick, and terra-cotta building is suitably imposing despite its narrow 50-foot width. Finished just as the 1920s land boom peaked, its height, design, and expensive materials imply power, prestige, and wealth. Classically inspired, the 3-story base includes granite pilasters with bronze relief spandrels in between and the building's name prominently displayed in the cornice above. The fourth floor is transitional. The building shaft then rises unadorned to express the steel-frame structure. The top of the building is its most distinctive feature: a 2-story copper-faced curved mansard roof with elaborate arched and bull's-eye windows inspired by French Second Empire architecture. If that were not enough, the final flourish is a domed, octagonal cupola. Miami had seen nothing else like it before, nor would it again. Robert Greenfield (1872–1938) was a prominent Buffalo, New York, architect and engineer with a wide-ranging practice, from designing churches to serving as a superintendent in the office of the U.S. Treasury Department, the agency then responsible for overseeing the design and construction of federal government buildings. Today the Security Building is a residential condominium.

118 NE 2nd Street
Orin T. Williams, 1925

Gesu Church is hard to miss. Located on a prominent downtown Miami corner, the rectangular stucco-covered building is large, distinctively designed,
and now painted bubble-gum pink. Henry Flagler donated the land in the
1890s for the construction of Holy Name Catholic Church (later renamed
Gesu) as part of what he envisioned as an Avenue of Churches in downtown Miami. It was Miami's first Catholic congregation. By 1920 the grow-
ing parish needed a larger church as well as a new rectory and school (now
demolished) and thus completed this complex. Parishioners enter the main
portal of the 4-story, 800-seat church on NE 1st Avenue through a deep
double-story arcaded portico divided into 3 bays. The north and longer
façade includes 8 tall arched panels, each containing polychromed crystal
leaded windows. Atop the orange Spanish barrel-tile roof and directly over
the narthex is an elaborate tower complex that steps back three times from
its rectangular base and includes an arched belfry. The elaborate interior
decoration combines features that include a mosaic dome, altars made of
Italian marble, and biblical scenes in the windows with elements reflecting
a changing congregation such as the mural over the main altar showing
Christ amidst a multicultural flock.

M1-27 CONGRESS BUILDING

111 NE 2nd Avenue
Martin Luther Hampton, 1923, 1926
Residential rehabilitation: Adolfo Albaisa, 1999

The 21-story Congress Building has an unusual construction history. It is two buildings in one, both designed by Martin Luther Hampton (1890–1950) and built three years apart. The original 5-story building features five double-story glass-arched openings on the ground floor with a single stylized roundel in between each one above the second level. Each of the bays on the next three stories has a set of three windows stacked one above the other and separated by a polychrome terra-cotta panel. Roped columns inspired by Spanish-Moorish architecture divide the windows. But a changed height limit in 1925 and a strong market encouraged further development in downtown Miami, so a tower was built above. It is comprised of two tall blocks with an additional level on the south wing because it includes an uppermost mechanical floor. To support the addition, structural engineer E. A. Sturman devised a truss system placed through the sixth and seventh floors that connects to the columns of the original building. The new floors are a straightforward grid of window and wall rising to a flat roof. Architect Hampton was talented and versatile (see MB1-12), not only designing commercial structures but also public buildings, country clubs, apartments, hotels, and homes.

TOUR 3: MIAMI 2

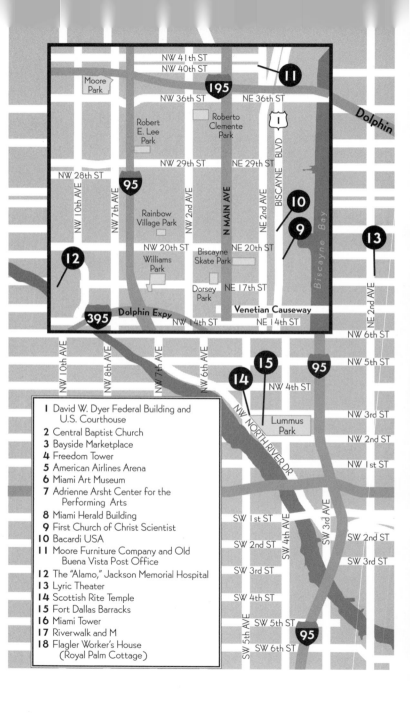

NW 41th ST
NW 40th ST

Moore
Park

11

195

NW 36th ST   NE 36th ST

Dolphin

Robert
E. Lee
Park

Roberto
Clemente
Park

1

NW 29th ST   NE 29th ST

NW 28th ST

95

NW 10th AVE
NW 7th AVE
NW 2nd AVE
N MAIN AVE
NE 2nd AVE
BISCAYNE BLVD

10

Rainbow
Village Park

9

Biscayne Bay

13

NW 20th ST   NE 20th ST

Williams
Park

Biscayne
Skate Park

12

Dorsey
Park

NE 17th ST

NE 2nd AVE

395

Dolphin Expy
NW 14th ST   NE 14th ST

Venetian Causeway

NW 6th ST

NW 10th AVE
NW 8th AVE
NW 7th AVE
NW 6th AVE

15

95

NW 5th ST

14

NW 4th ST

NW NORTH RIVER DR

NW 3rd ST

Lummus
Park

NW 2nd ST

NW 1st ST

1 David W. Dyer Federal Building and
U.S. Courthouse
2 Central Baptist Church
3 Bayside Marketplace
4 Freedom Tower
5 American Airlines Arena
6 Miami Art Museum
7 Adrienne Arsht Center for the
Performing Arts
8 Miami Herald Building
9 First Church of Christ Scientist
10 Bacardi USA
11 Moore Furniture Company and Old
Buena Vista Post Office
12 The "Alamo," Jackson Memorial Hospital
13 Lyric Theater
14 Scottish Rite Temple
15 Fort Dallas Barracks
16 Miami Tower
17 Riverwalk and M
18 Flagler Worker's House
(Royal Palm Cottage)

SW 1st ST
SW 4th AVE
SW 3rd AVE

SW 2nd ST   SW 2nd ST

SW 3rd ST   SW 3rd ST

SW 4th ST

SW 5th AVE   SW 5th ST

95

SW 6th ST

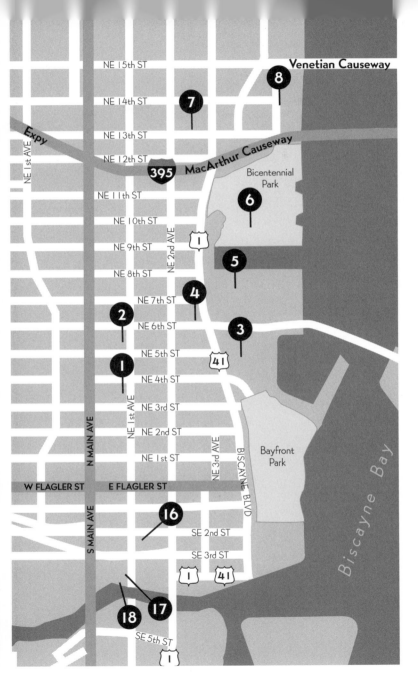

DAVID W. DYER FEDERAL BUILDING AND U.S. COURTHOUSE

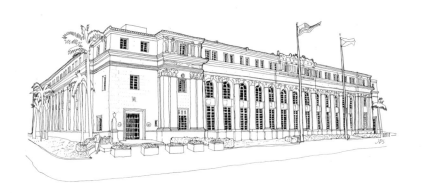

300 NE 1st Avenue
Paist & Steward with Marion Manley, 1933
Expansion: Spillis Candela & Partners, 1983

The construction of the U.S. Post Office and Courthouse was an important project for downtown Miami in the early 1930s during depressing economic times. Amid the gloom arose this large, 3-story limestone structure with an exterior of classical elements mixed with Mediterranean design and an elaborate interior featuring marble, gilt, leather doors, and crystal chandeliers. More restrained than its earlier counterpart (see M1-24), the exterior features a 2-story central bay that projects slightly and is composed of Corinthian columns that support a simple entablature and alternate with two levels of fenestration. At each end of the colonnade are bays with paired Corinthian columns. The north and south façades follow a similar rhythm with pilasters used instead of columns. The third floor is recessed and has smaller paired windows. Terra-cotta tiles cover a shallow hipped roof. The interior includes an open courtyard with arched entryways and a 2-story gallery. A 1983 addition that extended the building to a full city block includes a second courtyard. The building was renamed in honor of Judge Dyer, a former chief justice of the Southern District, in 1997. But today the structure lies abandoned, the result of air-contamination issues that forced tenant evacuation in 2008.

500 NE 1st Avenue
Dougherty and Gardner, 1926

Central Baptist Church was another recipient of Henry Flagler's ecclesiastical land largess (see M1-26, M2-9) for his "Avenue of Churches." But soon after the church was built on the donated lots, the congregation found a larger site a block away. There it moved, constructed a second church, and finally in 1926 completed this imposing, fortresslike edifice that hugs the sidewalk and sides of NW 1st Avenue between NE 5th and 6th Streets. Two identical projecting columned porticos with pediments, one facing south, the other east, dominate the restrained classical façade. Peeking above the 4-story mass is a polygonal rotunda capped by a cupola surfaced with gold leaf. The entire roof is covered with terra-cotta barrel tiles, a nod to southern Mediterranean aesthetic impulses. Inside, the 2,500-seat sanctuary, still among the largest assembly halls in the downtown area, dominates the spatial plan. Rooms off a perimeter ambulatory serve various church functions, including choir rehearsal spaces, classrooms and a library. Nashville-based Edward Emmett Dougherty (1876–1943) and Thomas W. Gardner (1882–1952) were well known as church architects having designed, among others, the First Baptist Church in Williamsburg, Kentucky (1926) and the Campbell-Eagan Educational Building for the Central Presbyterian Church in Atlanta (1925).

401 Biscayne Boulevard
Benjamin Thompson & Associates, 1987
Miamarina, Alfred Browning Parker, 1971

In the 1980s when Miami real estate was booming, the idea to develop a retail destination around the existing Bayfront Park marina, Miamarina, appealed to city boosters. It attracted the attention of the Rouse Company, which was best known for such inner-city "festival marketplaces" as Boston's Fanueil Hall (1974) and Baltimore's Harborplace (1980). The result was Bayside Marketplace, a roughly 250,000-square-foot indoor-outdoor complex comprised of twin 2-story metal-roofed long rectangular buildings that contain food, shopping, and display spaces connected to an open-air market with space for additional vendors. Bayside Marketplace has proved hugely popular for Miami's tourist industry drawing an average of 15 million visitors annually since it opened in 1987, including locals who enjoy live entertainment and tourists from nearby docked cruise lines. The architect was Benjamin Thompson (1918–2002), whose ideals of human scale and social activity informed his concept of creating "The City of Man." He first founded The Architects' Collaborative (TAC) with architect Walter Gropius (1883–1969) before establishing his own firm in 1967. Set along the Bay Biscayne ocean vista, the buildings act as a backdrop for the interaction of people enjoying their leisure time. Perhaps that is one secret of their success.

600 Biscayne Boulevard
Schultze and Weaver, 1925
Renovation: Rodriguez & Quiroga Architects, 2003
Historic name: Miami Daily News Tower

Looking for inspiration when his firm received major commissions in South Florida in the 1920s, designer Leonard Schultze was clearly taken by the Giralda Bell Tower in Seville, Spain, not once, but three times: the Freedom Tower, the Biltmore Hotel in Coral Gables, and the Roney Plaza Hotel in Miami Beach (demolished). The Freedom Tower came first and is the most elaborate. It was developed as the headquarters and printing plant of the *Miami Daily News*, Miami's oldest newspaper, after former Democratic presidential nominee James Cox purchased the paper in 1923. The entrance is marked with an arched doorway flanked by two columns that support a swan's-neck pediment with a richly decorated arched window set in-between, above, and a decorative stone escutcheon below. Set on a 3-story base, the 12-story tower is 3 bays wide and 3 bays deep with a 2-story setback at the upper level that is topped with an octagonal tower. In the 1960s, after the newspaper had moved out, this tall beacon on the bay became the site offering services for thousands of Cuban refugees. It was renamed Freedom Tower to honor that purpose. Today it is the home of Miami Dade College. Don't miss the New World mural inside.

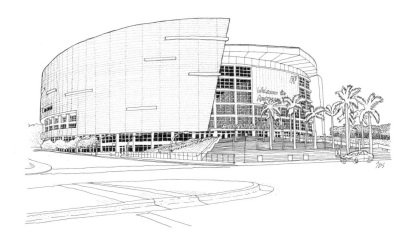

601 Biscayne Boulevard
Arquitectonica and Heinlein Schrock Stearns, 1999

The American Airlines Arena, located on Biscayne Boulevard overlooking the Port of Miami, serves as both a civic landmark and an entertainment center. It's easy to see why Bernardo Fort-Brescia, founder of Arquitectonica, says that his favorite view is from Biscayne Bay. The dynamic sweep of the curves that wrap the gridded stadium, the nautical references of sails and fins, and the broad terraces that beckon to the bay all suggest movement and pleasure whether looking at or from the structure. On the city side the 782,400-square-foot arena connects to Miami by the use of a grand staircase reaching to the sidewalk and the window wall that offers graphic media screens and interior views of activity, especially at night. But the concrete and glass exterior would mean little unless the interior met its primary function: to serve the Miami Heat NBA team by providing a main basketball court, practice and training facilities, management offices, and amenities for fans and visitors. So far, so good. Indeed, the spaces have proved so flexible that the Arena has become a popular destination for cultural and music events as well as sports. If flying over downtown Miami, look for the American Airlines airplane painted on the roof.

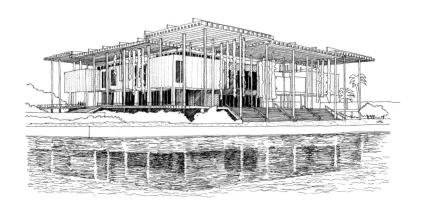

Museum Park, Biscayne Boulevard
Herzog & de Meuron Architekten, 2013

The Miami Art Museum's long anticipated move from Flagler Street (see M1-19) to the 40-acre waterfront site formerly known as Bicentennial Park aims not only to expand the museum's footprint but also to energize an underutilized downtown area as a cultural hub. The city's future plans call for a new science museum to share the park site. With climate in mind, Herzog & de Meuron's design for the 120,000-square-foot concrete and steel museum has a long, broad, shaded public terrace to transition between the park and the museum building. Slender columns, some covered with plants as a kind of hanging garden, offer structural support, add visual interest, and help bring the outdoors in. The museum is conceived as a complex of open spaces and gallery modules that encourage diverse viewing paths for visitors and flexible exhibition arrangements for curators. The 3-story building is topped with a flat reinforced-concrete roof punctuated with slits that filter Miami's strong sunlight to the spaces below. In addition to gallery space, the museum includes a library, auditorium, classrooms, workshop, offices, café, and museum shop. Herzog & de Meuron had built nothing in Miami prior to 2010. Now it has two very different structures to its credit (see MB2-17).

ADRIENNE ARSHT CENTER FOR THE PERFORMING ARTS

1300 Biscayne Boulevard
Cesar Pelli & Associates, 2006
Sears, Roebuck Building: Nimmons, Carr & Wright, 1929
Renovation of Sears, Roebuck Tower: R. J. Heisenbottle Architects, 2004

Miami's long-awaited performing arts center had mixed reviews when it opened in 2006, and the jury is still out. Critics cited project delays, cost overruns, inconvenient parking, and poor restaurant options, conditions in part outside the architect's purview. But the complex itself remains problematic. The 570,000-square-foot center is comprised of two huge cruise ship–like edifices docked opposite each other on Biscayne Boulevard. The purpose of a pedestrian bridge and a landscaped courtyard is to link the structures, but busy Biscayne Boulevard still keeps them apart. On the east side is the 2,200-seat John S. and James L. Knight Concert Hall and outreach facilities; on the west, the 2,400-seat Sanford and Dolores Ziff Ballet Opera House and 200-seat studio theater. Adjacent to the latter is a historic Art Deco tower, all that remains of the 1929 Sears, Roebuck & Company department store. The architects said that they designed the buildings without main entrances in order to better relate them to the surrounding neighborhood. Instead, this decision leaves the impression that these hulking masses are unanchored to the site, adrift with no "there" there. Yet the interiors of both the Concert Hall and the Opera House are stunning, flexible, and operationally successful spaces.

1 Herald Plaza
Naess & Murphy, 1960
North wing top floor addition: Frank Beas, 1984–88

Built over fifty years ago, the Miami Herald Building is a fine example of mid-century modern architecture in Miami. The property consists of three sections: the long bargelike office building, the adjacent originally window-less printing plant, and a parking garage integrated into the design. When the company moved to this highly visible site overlooking the city between the MacArthur and Venetian causeways, the 7-story, 758,000-square-foot building was the largest in Florida, with the most extensive printing plant facilities in the business. To design it the newspaper hired a Chicago firm, Naess & Murphy, which had recently completed the *Chicago Sun-Times* headquarters on the Chicago River with similar programmatic needs. Although the size, materials, and color schemes of the buildings differ, they are clearly related: both are 7-stories, share repetitive window-wall treatments, and have nearly identical massing. However, whereas the Sun-Times building is dark granite and aluminum, the Miami Herald Building uses a tropical color scheme for the façade: cool white Vermont marble to clad window piers and the solid south wall, gold-colored mosaic tile spandrels and, originally, pastel blue for the sunshade grilles of the windows. Note also that the main building is raised one story on pilotis to safeguard it from flooding.

FIRST CHURCH
OF CHRIST SCIENTIST

1836 Biscayne Boulevard
August Geiger, 1925

Christian Science churches throughout the country are designed in many different styles, but this Miami church is all about the classical. The imposing 2-story symmetrical structure uses granite from Mt. Airy, North Carolina, for the steps and water table and buff-colored Bedford, Indiana, limestone supplied by the Ingalls Stone Company for the building. The congregation, first organized in 1916, grew so quickly that within a decade it needed a facility that could seat 1,200 people. The church has a rectangular plan with a semicircular extension on the rear and extends from Biscayne Boulevard back to NE 2nd Court at 19th Street. The principal elevation faces Biscayne Boulevard and consists of 6 colossal Ionic columns that divide a recessed portico into 7 bays. On either side are end bays without any openings that connect to the rest of the structure by the entablature. A masonry parapet conceals the flat roof. The side elevation has tall multi-paned windows separated by pilasters, with shorter windows below that give light to the raised basement. The main auditorium is decorated with stylized classical motifs, has a shallow dome, and is accessed from the 5 double-entry doors in the recessed portico. Remarkably, the church remains virtually unaltered to this day.

2100 Biscayne Boulevard
Tower: Sacmag International, 1963; Annex: Ignacio Carrera-Justiz, 1973

Bacardi USA is quintessential Miami. It combines the young city's Mid-century Modern style with the artistic expressionism of its Latin culture. The complex consists of two structures linked by a plaza: an 8-story reinforced-concrete tower faced on the narrow north and south sides with 28,000 blue and white floral tiles designed by Brazilian artist Francisco Brennand (b. 1927) and a 2-floor square structure built ten years later by architect Ignacio Carrera-Justiz that is covered with a glass façade mural based on a painting by Johannes Dietz. The Bacardi Corporation valued fine design: its Mexico City offices were by Mies van der Rohe. Forced to relocate from Cuba, Bacardi sought a signature structure in Miami. Enrique Gutierrez's design is an homage to Mies, an engineering feat and an artistic triumph. The building consists of a ground-floor recessed glass lobby with a mirrored glass box above. The top floor is screened. The entire building is hung from concrete trusses that rest on four exterior columns, while steel cables on the end walls tie it together. Carrera-Justiz's addition is likewise impressive. Suspended 47 feet above the ground, floors are hung from the roof by 28 sensor rods supported by the reinforced-concrete central core.

M2-11 MOORE FURNITURE COMPANY AND OLD BUENA VISTA POST OFFICE

4040 NE 2nd Avenue
Exterior renovation: Architectural Design Consultants, 1992
Interior renovation: Walter F. Chatham, 1998

Buena Vista Post Office
4000 NE 2nd Avenue
1921

The design, location, and height of the 18,600-square-foot brick and terra-cotta Moore Building make it the centerpiece of the Miami Design District. It was built by "pineapple king"-farmer-turned-real-estate-developer Theodore Vivian Moore as a furniture store and stands at the commercial crossroads of the Buena Vista community that is now part of the City of Miami. Indeed, the L-shaped building faces both 40th Street and 2nd Avenue. Its large display windows and arched end bays make this 4-story building look imposing in this mainly low-rise neighborhood. Inside, the floors of the building wind around the skylit central atrium, creating an open, dramatic space for showcasing furniture then and providing a much-sought-after event venue now. In 2005, Design Miami honored architect Zaha Hadid (b. 1950) as Designer of the Year. In response, she created "Elastika," a permanent installation in the Moore Building that stretches white milled Styrofoam obliquely across the atrium to different floors, reminding some viewers of gum and others of marshmallow fluff. The crisp white neoclassical Buena Vista Post Office, now converted to a restaurant, occupies the actual corner of this enclave. Note the faded words "Post Office" and the federal eagle above the door.

THE "ALAMO," JACKSON MEMORIAL HOSPITAL

1611 Northwest 12th Avenue
August Geiger, 1918

Looking today more like a home than a hospital, the 14-bed City of Miami Hospital opened in June 1918, just in time to serve victims of the horrific flu pandemic. It was designed by August Geiger (1887–1968), the tenth registered architect in the state of Florida, who would have a highly successful career (see M1-18). Using a Mediterranean stylistic vocabulary that he is credited with introducing to South Florida, Geiger fashioned a 2½-story rectangular building made of reinforced concrete faced with creamy stucco and topped with an octagonal cupola and parapet-gable-ended red tile roof. The distinguishing features include the 1-story arcaded entrance veranda that extends across the façade, the three through-cornice dormers that echo the roofline parapets and finely crafted decorative roundels, carved faces, swirls, and swags that animate the surface. Nicknamed the "Alamo" for its resemblance to the Texas independence landmark, the hospital was renamed the Jackson Memorial Hospital in 1924 in honor of pioneer Miami physician Dr. James M. Jackson (see M1-6). Threatened by the construction of a maternal child-care center, it was saved in 1979 by moving it 475 feet. The Alamo now serves as a visitors' center for the University of Miami/Jackson Memorial Medical Center campus.

819 NW 2nd Avenue
c. 1913
Gedar Walker
Restoration: Beilinson Gomez Architects, 2000
Restoration and addition: R. J. Heisenbottle Architects with Judson Architecture, 2003

The Lyric Theater has a storied past but an uncertain future. The 2-story, 400-seat theater opened on January 14, 1914, the brainchild of Gedar Walker, a Georgia entrepreneur. Located on the street once called "Little Broadway," the theater catered to an African-American clientele in Miami's Overtown neighborhood and was considered among the finest theaters in the South. The exterior is largely intact. Two double-story pilasters flank the theater's wide arched entrance. In the center is a ticket booth with letters spelling "Lyric" on top. Two entry doors are on either side; above them are five glass panels. In the days of segregation, leading black artists who performed in Miami Beach but were not allowed to stay in hotels there would come back to Miami to play at the Lyric Theater. The theater came to symbolize the creative pulse of a vibrant neighborhood. After a long decline, the abandoned theater was targeted for renovation to help celebrate Miami's black history. A new 2-story glass-enclosed addition opened on the north side that offers a lobby space for patrons to mingle, a floating staircase, a café, and other amenities. Future plans call for extending the stage and upgrading the sound system. However, the project remains incomplete.

M2-14 SCOTTISH RITE TEMPLE

471 NW 3rd St
Kiehnel and Elliott, 1924

Sitting on a generous site overlooking the Miami River and opposite Lummus Park, the 3-story gray Scottish Rite Temple with its pyramid-shaped roof element looks formidable. Fierce double-headed eagles peer down from their roofline perch, keeping a watchful eye on all who enter past the four colossal Doric columns. If you do so, don't miss the compass and square on the wall above that symbolize the spiritual and physical linked together in Masonic brotherhood. The masonry structure, which is roughly T-shaped, with another entrance on North River Drive and a secondary entrance on 3rd Street, is even larger than it looks. It has 70 rooms, a commercial kitchen, 14 bathrooms, a library, and an ornate Egyptian-themed auditorium that with its two main balconies can seat up to 715 people. In the global fraternity of Freemasonry, different rites organizations exist that confer progressive decrees. In 1867, the Scottish Rite became the Supreme Council for the United States. The Miami Scottish Rite organization began in 1916. By the early twenties it was large and affluent enough not only to build this substantial Masonic temple but also to hire one of the leading architectural firms of the day, Kiehnel and Elliott, to design it.

Lummus Park, 404 NW 3rd Street
c. 1849
Exterior renovation: R. J. Heisenbottle Architects, 2000

The Fort Dallas Barracks has housed slaves, soldiers, stores, tourists, the Dade County government, an upscale tearoom, and artifacts of the American Revolutionary War. Built originally by slaves for slaves, it was saved from destruction in 1925 by the Daughters of the American Revolution who had it disassembled, reconstructed, and relocated from SE 1st Avenue and the Miami River to Lummus Park. Fort Dallas, named for Commodore James Dallas of the U.S. Navy, was established during the Second Seminole War (1835–38) near the mouth of the Miami River. William English acquired the land and brought slaves from North Carolina who were skilled stonemasons to construct the 95-by-17-foot 1-story building and a 2-story mansion (since demolished), both made of oolite rock, a kind of soft limestone found along the Florida coast. When the army returned during the Third Seminole War (1855–1858), the slave quarters became soldiers' barracks. In 1891, Miami pioneer Julia Tuttle bought the property, moved into the mansion, and renovated the barracks as tourist accommodations. The nearby Wagner Homestead (1855–58), originally on Wagner Creek, is the oldest known home still standing in Dade County. In 1979 the Dade Heritage Trust and the City of Miami moved it to the park.

M2-16 MIAMI TOWER

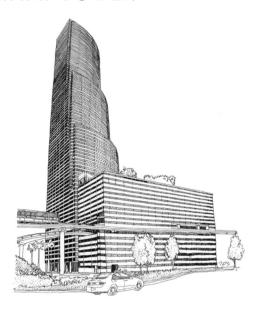

100 SE 2nd Street
Pei Cobb Freed & Partners, 1987
Formerly CenTrust, Bank of America at International Place, International Place

Built originally for CenTrust Bank, Miami Tower is an elegant solution for a small, complicated site. First of all, the 37-story, 600,000-square-foot sky-scraper had to be built atop an existing 10-story garage that abutted the elevated tracks of the Metromover. It also had to incorporate an elevated Metromover rail station, connect to the James L. Knight Center, and create a distinctive presence on the skyline without frontage on either Biscayne Bay or the Miami River. The architects' plan was to use only part of the garage roof as the base for the tower. Thus, the tower would not directly face the rail line and the remaining space could be used for a rooftop park. A handsome marble lobby on the 11th floor serves as a connecting hub for transit riders, office workers, and convention visitors. Three cascading curv-ing sections facing southeast give the glass tower identity; the backside of the building is straight. The *pièce de résistance* is a clever lighting system that allows each of the three tiers to be programmed differently. Colorful display options used for seasonal and other celebratory events continue to make Miami Tower a favorite city landmark. Attractive by day, it looks best at night.

88 SE 4th Street at Riverwalk Metromover Station
R&R Studios, 1996
Fort Dallas Park: Miami Riverwalk, ongoing

One of the most historic, and accessible, sections of Miami's riverfront is Fort Dallas Park. Blessed with a spectacular seaside setting, Miami was slow to see the 5.5-mile-long Miami River as a public amenity. But improvement plans spearheaded by the Miami River Commission and its partners are changing that perception. Today more than half of the public Miami River Greenway is either constructed or has fully funded plans to become so. The goal is to provide a continuous pedestrian pathway along the Miami River or adjacent roadway from the river's mouth at Biscayne Bay to the river's terminus at the Miami International Airport. The Riverwalk Metromover Station references that effort. A colossal red "M" designed by Roberto Behar and Rosario Marquardt marks the location of Miami's founder Julia Tuttle's home and doubles as a monument of Miami's centenary This 45-by-19-by-6-foot sculpture is an excellent example of the Miami-Dade County Art in Public Places program. It humanizes the 8-story Metromover access by offering a pedestrian pathway through the legs of the M and by its traditional, but oversized, pocket watch clock. The M is also symbolic and meant to encourage people to extend the letter into words of their choice.

M2-18 FLAGLER WORKER'S HOUSE (ROYAL PALM COTTAGE)

Fort Dallas Park, 60–64 SE 4th Street
Joseph A. McDonald, c. 1897

This little yellow house on Miami's Riverwalk is easy to miss in the shadow of high-rise developments all around it. Yet the building is a significant link to Miami's early days. It was one of at least 30 cottages built to house workers constructing the grand, exclusive Royal Palm Hotel (1897) being developed by railroad entrepreneur Henry Flagler the year after Miami became a city. Canadian Joseph McDonald (1842–1918), who oversaw construction of the Royal Palm Hotel, likely had these cottages built as well. The 2½-story clapboard structure is a common nineteenth-century American vernacular housing type but now so rare in Miami that this building is the last known example. Three bays wide, with a gable roof, the house includes a 1-story porch and windows with 6-over-6 lights on the front and 2-over-2 lights on the side flanked by shutters. In 1980, to prevent demolition, it was moved to Fort Dallas Park. This park was once the site of the United States military post established in 1836 on the plantation of Richard Fitzpatrick. Fort Dallas became the site for Miami's early development when pioneer Julia Tuttle renovated one of the fort's abandoned properties as her home (see M2-15).

TOUR 4: MIAMI BEACH 1 (SOUTH BEACH)

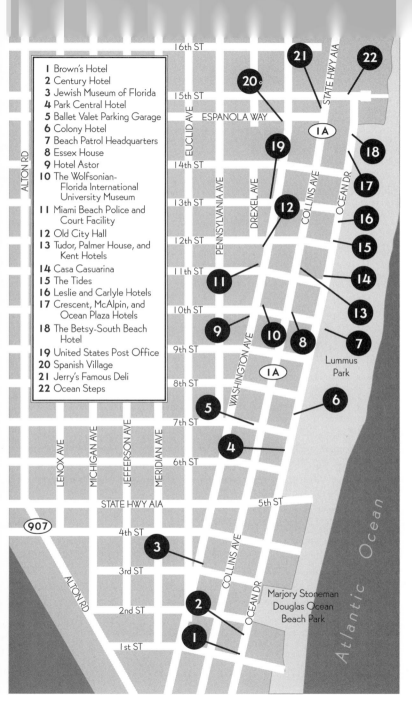

1 Brown's Hotel
2 Century Hotel
3 Jewish Museum of Florida
4 Park Central Hotel
5 Ballet Valet Parking Garage
6 Colony Hotel
7 Beach Patrol Headquarters
8 Essex House
9 Hotel Astor
10 The Wolfsonian-
   Florida International
   University Museum
11 Miami Beach Police and
   Court Facility
12 Old City Hall
13 Tudor, Palmer House, and
   Kent Hotels
14 Casa Casuarina
15 The Tides
16 Leslie and Carlyle Hotels
17 Crescent, McAlpin, and
   Ocean Plaza Hotels
18 The Betsy-South Beach
   Hotel
19 United States Post Office
20 Spanish Village
21 Jerry's Famous Deli
22 Ocean Steps

BROWN'S HOTEL

112 Ocean Drive
1915
Renovation and additions: Allan T. Shulman Architect, 2004

In 1915, when Scottish-born William J. Brown and his Irish wife Margaret opened the Atlantic Beach Hotel, the ocean lay directly before them past the boardwalk and beach. They set up the first floor for kitchens and cooking, the double-loaded second floor for bedrooms. The spot soon became known as Brown's Hotel. The long, rectangular 2-story structure is made of insect-resistant Dade County pine. It has wooden clapboard siding and a parapet roof with the hotel name front and center and rectangular "ears" on the ends. The façade is symmetrical: on the second level, a central hallway is flanked by 3 bays on either side; below is an enclosed, nearly square entry porch. Not long ago the building was an eyesore. Renamed the Star Apartments, it had become a dilapidated rental covered in thick stucco that hid its period features. In 2004 a careful renovation and integrated addition by architect Allan Shulman salvaged much historic fabric while updating the hotel. Nine rooms and suites were created on the second floor and a high-end restaurant fills the ground floor and patio. This little building has withstood hurricanes, defacement, derelicts, and development. Yet still it stands a century later, the first hotel in Miami Beach.

MB1-2 CENTURY HOTEL

140 Ocean Drive
Henry Hohauser, 1939
Renovation: Beilinson Architect, 1988

In 1932 architect Henry Hohauser moved to Miami Beach from New York, where he had been designing summer seaside bungalows in Far Rockaway, Queens. It was a smart career decision. Soon, facing the same ocean but a thousand miles south, he was designing hotels year-round. Hohauser is credited with more than 200 buildings in Miami Beach. In the process he helped create a distinctively tropical Art Deco style—modern, cheerful, and clever. Hohauser is clearly comfortable working at a small scale. The 2-story Century Hotel containing 31 rooms is a good example since it retains much of the original design. Horizontal and vertical elements play off each other on the symmetrical façade. Awning windows at the edges of each level emphasize the horizontality of the building, as does the architectural lettering of the hotel's name spelled out in neon above the entry. The windows have "eyebrows" that offer shade and give dimensionality to the building. Above them at the roofline are three circles that suggest ship portholes. Then, rising from the eyebrow of the center awning windows is a bold vertical beacon with horizontal bands of neon that gives the hotel a theatrical glow at night and an unmistakable identity.

301 Washington Avenue
Henry Hohauser, 1936
Renovation and adaptive use: Giller &
Giller, 1993

Temple Beth Jacob
311 Washington Avenue
H. Frasser Rose, 1929
Schoolroom addition: Robert Swartburg,
1946

Two synagogues designed at different times by different architects have been restored and transformed into the Jewish Museum of Florida to honor the history of Jews in the state. The location is no accident. In the 1920s Jews were not allowed to live north of 5th Street. Temple Beth Jacob at 311 Washington Avenue was the first synagogue built in Miami Beach. Little is known of the architect, but he created a lovely symmetrical design. Two-story triple arches flanked by small circular windows mark the stucco façade. Each arch contains dark double wooden entrance doors with an arched window above. At the peak of the roof is a tablet of the Ten Commandments. Seven years later, noted architect Henry Hohauser (1885–1963), a member of the congregation, designed a larger, more ornate synagogue next door that references the earlier temple in its gable-roofed rectangular form and other elements. A large single arch in the center frames the entrance, with doors below and stained glass above. Narrow 2-story arched windows are placed on either side of the doorway and a shallow copper dome rises from the sanctuary. Special features include over 80 stained-glass windows, a marble bimah, and numerous Art Deco details.

MB1-4 PARK CENTRAL HOTEL

640 Ocean Drive
Henry Hohauser, 1937
Renovation: Beilinson Architect, 1988

Locals call the Park Central Hotel the "Blue Jewel" and for good reason. At 7 stories, it rises among its neighbors as one of the tallest Art Deco hotels on Ocean Drive, and its blue-shaded center section is unmistakable. Park Central, spelled out in stainless-steel letters on the entrance canopy, evokes both the hotel's site across from Lummus Park and a handsome 1920s Manhattan counterpart near Central Park with the same name. Multipaned rectangular windows that turn the corner at the edge of each floor act as decorative features on the crisp two-toned blue and white symmetrical façade. Portholes, a typical Miami Beach Art Deco element, add a nautical theme on the second floor. Quality materials and details enhance the interior. The decorative lobby floor is made of terrazzo, a compound of cement and stone chips that can be colored, poured, and polished. Look for the PC logo near the reception desk or, up the stairs, the view from the octagonal portholes. Early on, the hotel's service and style attracted Hollywood celebrities. Later, although faded, the Park Central still retained a stylish presence. No wonder it was among the first hotels to be renovated in the resurgence of Miami Beach in the 1980s.

MB1-5 BALLET VALET PARKING GARAGE

210 7th Street
Exterior Design: Arquitectonica, 1996
Architect and Structural Engineer: Desman Associates, 1996

Inventive parking garage design may not immediately come to mind when thinking of a beachfront resort community but Miami Beach offers examples by two of the best firms practicing in the world today: Herzog & de Meuron's 1111 Lincoln Road (see MB2-17) and Arquitectonica's Ballet Valet Parking Garage completed fifteen years earlier. Arquitectonica's challenge was to screen a six-level, 234,000-square foot parking structure for 646 cars in a way that was functional, attractive, and complementary to the Art Deco storefronts façades below that had been saved in an historic preservation compromise. To do so, the design architects turned to nature. They devised a fiberglass trellis integrated into the upper parking levels to support perimeter planters that surround the edges of each floor. Three different plants, all tropical shrubs, provide different shades of green: *Clusia guttifera*, *Conocarpus erectus*, and *Scaevola frutescans*. The greenery was planted to grow in the shape of layered green waves along the sides of the structure, thus recalling the nearby ocean while hiding ugly mechanical systems and absorbing carbon dioxide. The plants, however, have been so happy in their sunlit, well-watered parking garage environment, that instead of behaving properly manicured, they have spilled out over the edges in a much more untamed South Beach way.

COLONY HOTEL

736 Ocean Drive
Henry Hohauser, 1935
Renovation: Moshe Cosicher, 1989

The 3-story Colony was among the first hotels completed by Henry Hohauser in Miami Beach, and he made sure it would not go unnoticed. Envisioned as a theatrical façade, the name is boldly displayed in large letters on three sides of a bladelike marquee that ends with the word "Hotel" over the entrance. Add neon and it's easy to see why the Colony remains one of the most photographed hotels in South Beach. The inverted T design divides the façade into two equal parts. On the upper floors windows squarely turn the corners, but the concrete sunshades above them have rounded edges. On the second and third floors the marquee is flanked by a window with a stack of horizontal painted lines beneath it. This motif ends with vertical lines at the roofline. Finally, a thin wavy line runs across the top of the building. But don't miss the inside. There you'll find a striking floor-to-ceiling accordion-pleated fireplace made of pale green structural glass, called Vitrolite or Carrera depending upon the manufacturer. Note the painting by Paul Simone of tequila cultivation in northern Mexico that includes a man and two statuesque women standing in a field with horses and cacti beyond.

MB1-7 BEACH PATROL HEADQUARTERS

1001 Ocean Drive
Robert A. Taylor, 1939
Oceanfront Auditorium, Leonard Glasser, 1954
Renovation: STA Architectural Group, 2009

The Beach Patrol Headquarters may be South Beach's most iconic structure. Designed by Robert A. Taylor (see MB1-20) to resemble the stern of an ocean liner, it sits so close to the water that it could almost float, and its portholes, ship railings, and mastlike flagpole reflect an appropriate nautical Art Deco style. But the building is more than an architectural folly. The 3,369-square-foot building serves as the hub for the Miami Beach ocean rescue teams, which officially began their work in 1926. In 1954, Leonard Glasser (1922–1982) completed the Miami Modern (MiMo) Oceanfront Auditorium, which faces Ocean Drive, and connected it to the Beach Patrol Headquarters for their use as well. The city recently completed a renovation, reconstruction, and expansion project for the complex that included renovating the Beach Patrol building, separating the structures to allow a pathway between them for continuous pedestrian access through Lummus Park and constructing an addition to the Auditorium building while retaining its 1950s character. The 17,000-square-foot building, home to the Miami Design Preservation League offices and gift shop, now includes a glass-walled 2-story, 4,000-square-foot exhibit and assembly area as well as upgraded space for ocean rescue operations.

MB1-8 ESSEX HOUSE

1001 Collins Avenue
Henry Hohauser, 1938

It is said that during the boom time of the late 1930s as many as 100 hotels a year were built in Miami Beach: the 3-story peach-colored Essex House is one of the best. With this corner site, Hohauser could enhance a streamlined look by using both façades in a continuous curve. Each end of the building is rounded, as is the entry itself. The simplified form becomes a canvas on which to display elements of the Moderne stylistic language: concrete sunshades; the neon-lettered hotel name; raised striping lines repeated to convey movement; portholes to suggest ocean liner travel, and at the corner, a tall finial proclaiming the hotel name. As with the Park Central (see MB1-4), the Essex House recalls the name of a famous Manhattan hotel. Unlike many renovated hotels, the interior lobby of the Essex House retains much original material. Note especially the original Earl LePan mural of Indians in the Everglades and the little alligator he added fifty years later; the etched-glass door of palms and flamingos on the porch side, and the arrow on the terrazzo floor pointing to a tiny bar. Legend has it that mobster Al Capone played poker in the secret lounge here.

MB1-9 HOTEL ASTOR

956 Washington Avenue
T. Hunter Henderson, 1936
Renovations and addition: Kobi Karp Architecture & Interior Design, 1993

Kitty-corner from the Wolfsonian Museum (see MB1-10) on busy Washington Avenue sits the understated Hotel Astor. It doesn't call attention to itself with colorful details or try to go somewhere with streamlined movement but rather commands attention by simply standing still. Quality materials and fine proportions help. The building is a 7-bay-wide cube with a recessed L wing to the south. Its lower third is faced with keystone, an abundant coral rock in Florida containing fossilized shells and plants that architects liked to use because it is easily cut and colored. Here it is pale pink with gray bands inserted to continue the lines of door panels and first-floor windows. The entrance, set back from the street, is framed with trimmed hedges. Note the words "Hotel Astor" and the striped pavement at the entry. White curved and fluted pilasters flank the double entry doors. The second- and third-story end bays have sunshades, but otherwise the windows are plain elongated rectangles. A pierced masonry screen atop the parapet adds a decorative element to draw our eyes upward. T. Hunter Henderson designed nearly thirty buildings in Miami Beach from 1929 to 1964, but he is best known for the Hotel Astor, where he got everything right.

THE WOLFSONIAN-FLORIDA INTERNATIONAL UNIVERSITY MUSEUM

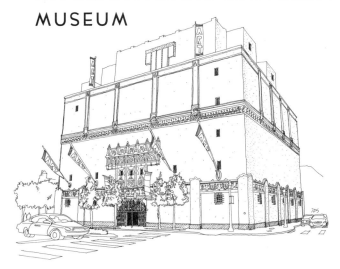

1001 Washington Avenue
Robertson & Patterson, 1927; Addition: Robert M. Little, 1936
Renovation, Hampton & Kearns, 1992
Originally Washington Storage Company

In a way, 1001 Washington has always collected the familiar. The original 3-story structure was completed a year after the 1926 hurricane as a place for seasonal Miami Beach residents to safely store their belongings. It was deliberately designed as almost windowless but is hardly nondescript. The architects, who had recently finished Temple Israel in Miami, embellished the plain white surface with two bands of ornate gold-colored Spanish-Moorish carved ornament and a similarly inspired T-shaped flourish over the doorway. In 1936, architect Robert M. Little added two stories. When Wometco company heir Mitchell Wolfson, Jr., purchased the building to house his collection of material culture, additional work was required. From 1988 to 1992, Hampton & Kearns enlarged and renovated the structure, transforming it into a 7-story, 56,000-square-foot public museum now owned by Florida International University. Note the T repeated on the upper story and how interior details immediately envelope the visitor in a world of art and design. The collection, focused on artifacts from 1885 to 1945, aims to create a narrative that shows design as an active agent in human affairs. Don't miss the carved ceiling on the 7th floor taken from a local car dealership that cleverly incorporates automotive motifs.

MIAMI BEACH POLICE AND COURT FACILITY

1100 Washington Avenue
Jaime Borrelli and Markus Frankel and Peter Blitstein, 1987

Although invisible now, the planning and construction of this large public project was both complicated and controversial. The program called for a new police headquarters with a complex mix of operational systems, administrative functions, public safety training areas, and crime-related facilities; a 95,000-square-foot ramped parking garage; and the renovation of the old City Hall next door for courtrooms and other uses. Second, the project involved working with multiple municipal and county agencies with different needs, personnel, and time frames. Finally, a design-by-committee structure was put in place in which principals of three separate firms, Jaime Borrelli, Markus Frankel, and Peter Blitstein shared responsibility. Controversy ensued when the requirement that the police headquarters be adjacent to Old City Hall necessitated the demolition of a block of historic structures including a hotel designed by noted architect Henry Hohauser. Despite these obstacles, the new headquarters fits into its neighborhood context and functions well. Its low-rise scale helps its bulk blend with the surroundings, and the curving glass and sand-finished stucco exterior still looks fresh twenty-five years later. Old City Hall remains (see MB1-12) and the architects were even able to create a landscaped plaza amenity behind the building to connect the old and new.

MB1-12 OLD CITY HALL

1130 Washington Avenue
Martin Luther Hampton, 1927
Renovations: City of Miami Beach, 1993, 1999, 2006

Miami Beach citizens are proud of Old City Hall and they've spent their tax dollars to prove it. It was built after the 1926 hurricane, not only to replace a smaller facility located at 607 Collins Avenue but also to help restore confidence at a time of loss. Designed in the prevailing Mediterranean Revival mode, its central 5-bay-wide, 9-story stucco-surfaced tower is tastefully adorned with a few urns and columns and flanked by two 2-story wings on Washington Avenue. All roofs are tiled in red barrel clay. Using a few key forms, the approach is symmetry, repetition, and restraint. Note how the multipaned arched windows at the base are echoed on the top story and again with blind arches above on the square cupola. Hampton had a fine sense of proportion and a flourishing design practice. Although the municipal government moved to a new City Hall in 1977 (see MB2-14), the plan also required the renovation of the older building for new tenants. Recently, an even more extensive renovation was completed, including hurricane protection, structural repairs, and restorative interior work in the lobby and elsewhere. Indeed, Old City Hall may be in better shape now than when it was new.

TUDOR, PALMER HOUSE, AND KENT HOTELS

Tudor Hotel & Suites
1111 Collins Avenue
L. Murray Dixon, 1939
Rooftop addition: Max Wolfe Sturman,
2007

Palmer House Hotel
1119 Collins Avenue
L. Murray Dixon, 1939
Renovation and addition: Max Wolfe
Sturman, 2007

Kent Hotel
1131 Collins Avenue
L. Murray Dixon, 1939
Renovation and addition: Giller & Giller,
2005

L. Murray Dixon (1901–1949) was a busy man in 1939, designing, among his many other projects, these three adjacent hotels on a single block. Indeed, Dixon may have been the city's most prolific architect working in the 1930s and 1940s, designing more than 40 hotels as well as residences, apartment buildings, stores, and interiors. This particular trio shows how Dixon mixed and matched stylistic language and forms he had helped popularize in Miami Beach. The 3-story Tudor Hotel on the far corner sets the stage as the largest and most prominently sited building. Dixon uses pink keystone effectively around the entry doors and in three wide curved bands above that correspond to floor levels. A tall spiral with the hotel's name continues from a center pilaster extending high above the roofline. Wings on either side together with two rows of sun-shaded windows add horizontality. The 3-story asymmetrical Palmer House uses similar sunshades, but its windows are continuous, and raised stripes draw attention to the vertical hotel marquee. The Kent Hotel, the most Modernist of the three, likewise uses asymmetry, ribbon windows, and sunshades but also employs round portholes as decorative devices in the entry. The small vertical roofline signage slices between the horizontal and vertical bays.

MB1-14 CASA CASUARINA

1114 Ocean Drive
Harry La Pointe and Arthur Laidler-Jones, 1930
Adaptive use, renovation, and south wing additions: Hawrylewicz & Robertson, 1993

The Casa Casuarina is a handsome 3-story courtyard mansion with a tragic history. The 13,250-square-foot house was built by Standard Oil heir Alden Freeman in 1930 and subsequently expanded another 6,100 square feet by its owner, designer Gianni Versace, who was murdered on the front steps in 1997. Freeman, who was known to dress up as Christopher Columbus, reportedly requested his architects to base their design on the 1510 Alcázar de Colón in Santo Domingo, the palace of Christopher Columbus's son, now a UNESCO World Heritage Site. But there is little apparent resemblance to the large arcaded fortress. The Casa's design was more likely inspired by the prevailing Mediterranean style of the day in Miami Beach: a pale or pastel flat-stuccoed façade, clay barrel tile roof, iron balconies, and punched-out arched and rectangular windows. In 1993, Versace received permission to demolish the Revere Hotel next door, allowing him space to construct a double-story arcaded wing, pool and garden, and garage. Some say that the mansion's name honors the casuarina tree, many of which were planted in Miami Beach by pioneer John Collins; others claim that Freeman was inspired by a W. Somerset Maugham collection of short stories titled *The Casuarina Tree* (1926).

1220 Ocean Drive
L. Murray Dixon, 1936
Renovation: Mosscrop Associates, 1997

A sense of urbanity came to the seashore when the Tides Hotel opened in 1936. At 10 stories high, the hotel rose above its neighbors. Its setbacks, scale, style, and masonry surface suggest high-rise prototypes. The hotel sits on two oceanfront lots totaling 13,000 square feet that the Lum family purchased from the U.S. government in 1883. Three years later they built their home there, the first one in Miami Beach. Dixon takes advantage of the site by setting back the hotel entry and creating a broad terrace as a place to see and be seen. A talented jazz musician as well as a gifted architect, Dixon had a rhythmic sense evident in the entrance, with its interplay of shapes and forms. The design is a kind of oversized tic-tac-toe configuration divided into rectangles by vertical and horizontal dividers and framed by a keystone rectangle. Each of three doorways is identical. Read vertically, they are composed of a double door, a porthole set within a solid keystone rectangle, and a multipaned window above that continues the third-floor fenestration line. The 7-bay façade rises smoothly from the street, is punctuated by a regular window pattern, and steps back above the 9th floor.

LESLIE AND CARLYLE HOTELS

Leslie Hotel
1244 Ocean Drive
Albert Anis, 1937
Renovation: Mosscrop Associates, 1996

The Carlyle
1250 Ocean Drive
Kiehnel and Elliott, 1939
Restoration and rooftop addition: Blake Thorson, 2002

Standing on the same Ocean Drive block, the Leslie and Carlyle hotels show how two talented architects interpret a common style. Born in Chicago, Albert Anis (1889–1964) developed a successful design practice in Miami Beach in the 1930s that comprised both commercial buildings and a dozen hotels. He divides the white, 3-story Leslie Hotel into 5 bays by a central section with vertical accordion walls painted yellow that flank bay windows. Two multipaned rectangular windows are on either side. Window eyebrows and the façade-wide entry canopy are painted yellow, thus drawing the eye to these horizontal elements. Above the door sleek silver architectural letters spell "Leslie." Classically trained designer Richard Kiehnel was born in Germany and worked in a variety of styles, often on large-scale projects including Mediterranean Revival estates for the wealthy and the Scottish Rite Temple (see M2-14). Three vertical shafts form the centerpiece of the slightly wider 3-story Carlyle Hotel. They rise from the entrance canopy, extend above the roof and terminate in Kiehnel's signature pierced masonry panels. The windows and their wide eyebrows turn the corner, giving the white façade a slightly streamlined look as does the script font used for "The" in the hotel's name.

CRESCENT, McALPIN, AND OCEAN PLAZA HOTELS

Crescent Hotel
1420 Ocean Drive
Henry Hohauser, 1938
Renovation: Beilinson Architect, 1988
Renovation and rooftop addition: James Silver with Allan T. Shulman Architect, 1999

McAlpin Hotel
1424 Ocean Drive
L. Murray Dixon, 1940
Renovation: Nichols, Brosch, Sandoval & Associates, 1999

Ocean Plaza Hotel
1430 Ocean Drive
L. Murray Dixon, 1941
Renovation: Beilinson Architect, 1990
Nichols, Brosch, Sandoval & Associates, 1999

All hotels: Hilton Resorts

These three hotels, related but different, sit like siblings on a block of Ocean Drive. Henry Hohauser's Crescent Hotel is the oldest. Its asymmetrical façade separates it from most of its extended Art Deco family. A vertical cane-shaped band curves at the roofline to divide the façade into 3 bays, 2 on the left and 1 on the right. A railroad-track motif next to it turns to run parallel to and just below the roofline. Window eyebrows, the porch canopy, and a line of graduated disks below the roof add horizontal elements. Some say that a tower was once planned for the building, which might account for its unusual design. Next door the McAlpin, designed by L. Murray Dixon two years later, shares the same height, eyebrow, and window lines, but is boxier and symmetrical. Windows turn the corner but there are no curves. A central post reaches from the second floor to an open rooftop pavilion. Finally, the 3-story Ocean Plaza, also by Murray, is the youngest, plainest, and flattest. Here he maintains the same window line, but eyebrows have disappeared and the windows themselves have become ribbons. A rooftop T indented into a shallow projecting square is the central focus.

THE BETSY-SOUTH BEACH HOTEL

1440 Ocean Drive
L. Murray Dixon, 1940–42
Renovation: Diamante Pedersoli and Carmelina Santoro with Beilinson Gomez Architects, 2008
Historic name: Betsy Ross Hotel

At first glance, the all-white Betsy Hotel South Beach seems a misfit among its Art Deco neighbors, but architect L. Murray Dixon, who was born in Live Oak, Florida, and graduated from the Georgia Institute of Technology, was so versatile and talented an architect that he could work well in a variety of styles. Inspired by American domestic architecture, he designed this hotel to recall gracious southern plantations as well as northern colonial houses, thus appealing to a geographically diverse clientele. Dixon takes full advantage of the ample street frontage on Ocean Drive by creating a wide 5-bay, 2-story columned porch flanked by projecting 3-bay gable-ended sections facing the street. Other colonial elements include fanlights, multipaned fenestration, a broken-pediment motif over the front door, and window shutters. The hotel was named for heroine Betsy Ross, a Philadelphia seamstress who sewed American flags—although historians say not the very first one. The patriotic connection continued during World War II when the U.S. Army brought recruits to Miami Beach for basic training and some lucky ones were housed in the hotel. Recently renovated, the interior has been elegantly updated and serves not only as a lobby but also as a salon programmed with community cultural events.

MB1-19 UNITED STATES POST OFFICE

1300 Washington
Howard Lovewell Cheney, 1937
Renovation: General Services Administration, 1977

This United States Post Office is a rare example in Miami Beach of a spare, simplified Art Moderne style. With minimal ornament or decoration, the building's appeal relies upon its form, siting, color, materials, scale, texture, and proportions. The plan hinges around a 2+-story central cylinder topped with a circular cupola that is flanked by 1-story asymmetrical wings. A tall central doorway has gridded glass above and a lone eagle signifying that this is a federal building. Silver letters spell out "United States Post Office" under the curved roof rim. Attached planters on either side of the door hold palm trees that add color and texture to the plain white surface of the building. Shallow steps made of pink marble gently lead from the corner sidewalk to the entry, which is outlined, as are all the windows and the roof edge itself, with the same stone. Though a building sprawls behind it, the façade is human-scale. Inside the circular lobby are three handsome murals of buff-bodied Spanish explorers and natives by Charles Russell Hardman and a sunray light fixture hanging from a teal-colored heavenly ceiling. Cheney's work is noteworthy, and several of his buildings are listed on the National Register of Historic Places.

1434–1440 Washington Avenue and 400–517 Espanola Way
Robert A. Taylor et al., 1925

Espanola Way may look like a Hollywood stage set, but it is one of the most intact mixed-use historic sections in Miami Beach. In 1922, William F. Whitman purchased land that lay at the northern edge of the community first platted as Ocean Beach and called it "Whitman's Spanish colony." Three years later, Newton Baker Taylor (N.B.T.) Roney purchased the property, consisting of 20 corner lots and 40 inside building lots, and formed the Spanish Village Corporation. He envisioned creating a bohemian artists' colony like Greenwich Village in Manhattan but with a Latin flair, hiring architect Robert A. Taylor to do so for the block between Washington and Drexel avenues. Taylor borrowed freely from French and Spanish seaside architecture, using thick stuccoed walls, large overhangs, bracketed balconies, archways, ironwork, carved wood, and other elements to construct the buildings that give the street a cohesive scale and style. Through the years the street continued to develop, becoming more residential toward the west. Although most people experience Espanola Way beginning at Washington Avenue, the official Espanola Way Historic District starts at Collins Avenue as a transitional commercial entrance and ends with residences at Jefferson Avenue. Peach-colored buildings with green-striped awnings add to the quaint, charming atmosphere.

1450 Collins
Henry Hohauser, 1939
Renovation: Charles H. Benson & Associates, 2001
Historic name: Hoffman's Cafeteria

Known originally as Hoffman's Cafeteria, this streamlined classic has returned to its roots as a casual restaurant after some wild club years. The building includes so many references to ocean liner imagery that the style is sometimes dubbed "Nautical Moderne." Note the roofline "portholes." the center "smokestack," and the long, wide horizontal "shiplap" siding on the wings and columns. But Hohauser is not simply using stylistic appliqué. He is showing us how to turn a corner in a sculptural way that goes beyond the simple smoothness of his slightly earlier Essex House nearby (see MB1-8), while the façade plays with solids and voids formed by rectangles, squares, circles, and cylinders. He uses all these elements to reinforce the "corner-ness" of the site as the vertical climax of the composition. Round-banded columns flank the double-door entry, becoming horizontal pylons above the curved entrance canopy. A flat, elongated flagpole holder lies at the center of each pylon, where flags and flagpoles draw the eye further upward. Directly above the entry is a tall curved pilaster with the name " Jerry's" that rises above a wide cylinder. Finally, three circles in descending size bring the eye back to the side wings, the sidewalk, and the viewer.

MB1-22 OCEAN STEPS

1500 Ocean Drive
Michael Graves & Associates 1995/1999

Legendary Ocean Drive ends at 15th Street in a 3-story horseshoe-shaped 53,000-square-foot shopping mall called Ocean Steps that was originally supposed to connect to the Royal Palm Resort (see MB2-1). This retail segment is part of a complex developed in the mid-1990s at Collins Avenue, 15th Street, and Ocean Drive that includes office, parking, retail, and residential components with overall design by architect Michael Graves (b. 1934). On the west end, Albert Anis's 1939 Bancroft Hotel on the corner of 15th and Collins was retained, although it lost its east and north façades and was partially eviscerated for commercial space and parking. On the east end, Graves designed a 15-story luxury residential tower containing 111 units, the last section a cylinder facing the beach directly, the first a rectangular volume oriented west toward downtown Miami. Graves relates to the historic 1930s neighborhood by using a peach and aqua palette and signature Art Deco shapes such as porthole circles. The Ocean Steps shopping area links these different components. Flanking the wide broad steps from Ocean Drive are two 2-story raised circular pavilions with 2 levels of retail shops attached that border the central plaza at the head of the stairs.

TOUR 5: MIAMI BEACH 2

B i s c a y n e   B a y

195   112   JULIA TUTTLE CAUSEWAY

1 Royal Palm Resort
2 Loews Miami Beach and
   St. Moritz Hotels
3 The Ritz Plaza Hotel
4 The Delano
5 Fontainebleau Hotel
6 Helen Mar
7 2228 Park Avenue
8 Bass Museum of Art
9 Albion Hotel
10 Temple Emanu-El
11 Fillmore East Miami Beach at the
   Jackie Gleason Theater
12 Miami Beach Convention Center
13 Miami Beach Community Church
14 Miami Beach City Hall
15 New World Symphony Center
16 Lincoln Road Mall
17 1111 Lincoln Road
18 Publix on the Bay
19 Flagler Memorial

18

20th ST

907

18th ST

DADE BLVD

VENETIAN CAUSEWAY

BAY RD

WEST AVE

ALTON RD

LENOX AVE

19

16th ST

17

15th ST

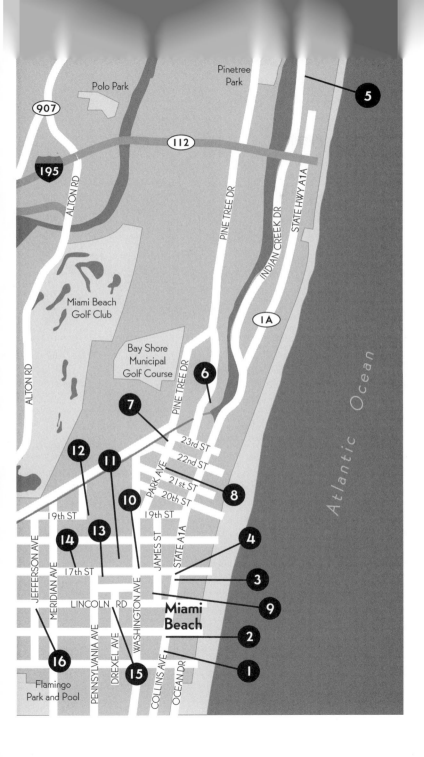

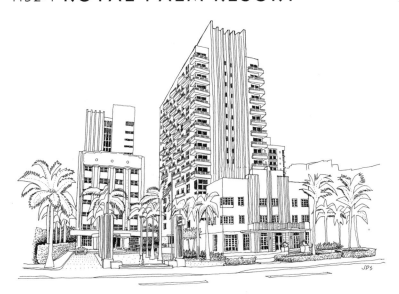

1545 Collins Avenue
Shorecrest Hotel façade: Kiehnel & Elliott, 1940
Royal Palm Hotel: Donald G. Smith, 1939
Towers and lanai: Arquitectonica additions, 2002

The Royal Palm South Beach Resort consists of five buildings: the 7-story Royal Palm and addition, the 15-story Shorecrest Hotel and addition, and an all-suites poolside lanai. The project was a complicated one for the city, the developer, and the Arquitectonica architectural team. It began in the 1990s, when the City of Miami Beach sought to redress past racial bias by encouraging African-American ownership in the hospitality industry. The Peebles Corporation won the bid to develop the 7-story historic Royal Palm Hotel property and also purchased the adjacent 1930s Shorecrest Hotel. When the Royal Palm turned out to have severe structural damage resulting from chlorine-contaminated concrete used during its 1930s construction, the building had to be destroyed. But mindful of historic preservation concerns, the city also required the developer to reconstruct the hotel using original plans and construction methods. Arquitectonica undertook this reconstruction as well as the renovation of the Shorecrest Hotel. Rear sections of both hotels were removed so that Arquitectonica could add a 17-story tower to each that faces the ocean: an angular addition to the Royal Palm and a glass circular tower to the Shorecrest. The lanai provides a connecting element to the site while adding stylistic panache.

LOEWS MIAMI BEACH AND ST. MORITZ HOTELS

Lowes Miami Beach Hotel	St. Moritz Hotel
1601 Collins Avenue	1565 Collins Avenue
Nichols, Brosch, Sandoval & Associates,	Roy F. France & Company, 1939
1998	Renovation: Zyscovich Architects

Conceived as part of the redevelopment plan for the Convention Center expansion (see MB2-15), Loews was the first major hotel built in Miami Beach in 30 years. The city requirements were twofold: construct a large, business-functional but family-friendly hotel and renovate an abandoned one next door, the St. Moritz. The combination may seem like odd bedfellows, but it works. The architectural firm now known as NBWW specializes in large projects. It softened the broad mass of the 18-story, 790-room Loews hotel by designing a 5-bay curved entrance at street level that continues the full height of the structure and is capped by a cupola ending in a slender lantern. Set back from the street, Roy France's 12-story angular, asymmetrical St. Moritz acts as an Art Deco exclamation point to its hefty neighbor. Its central vertical planes culminate in a tower block with an elongated recessed rectangle that is lit at night. Roy France (1888–1972), born in the small town of Hawley, Minnesota, trained at the Armour Institute of Technology (now ITT) and worked in Chicago designing apartments before moving to Miami Beach in the 1930s. He, Henry Hohauser, and L. Murray Dixon are the talented triumvirate responsible for many of Miami Beach's best historic buildings.

THE RITZ PLAZA HOTEL

1701 Collins Avenue
L. Murray Dixon, 1940
Renovation: Beilinson Architect, 1990
Historic name: Grossinger Beach Hotel

When the Ritz Plaza opened in 1946 as Grossinger's Beach Hotel, rooms were $6 a night including breakfast and dinner, an affordable rate meant to attract new business as well as to appeal to the Miami Beach clientele who had frequented Grossinger's famous Catskill resort in upstate New York. The 12-story structure is considered one of L. Murray Dixon's best expressions of the high-rise form. While its grid of solid and void, window and wall, can be seen in countless apartment buildings and skyscrapers, Dixon adds subtlety to the massing by the use of stepped vertical planes echoed in the ziggurat roofline silhouette and interest to the façade by vertical striping on the south side. But what also makes this building special is the way it reaches for the sky. The front of the hotel facing Collins Avenue includes piers flanking the central windows that stretch beyond the roofline. The *pièce de résistance* is the glorious tripartite glass-block lantern that hides the elevator shaft at the top. Here color, banding, light, and glass all come together in a fitting burst of energy. If renovations proceed as planned, the Ritz Plaza will once again rejoin its neighbors as a Miami Beach icon.

THE DELANO

1685 Collins Avenue
B. Robert Swartburg, 1947
Renovation: Philippe Starck, 1994

The Delano Hotel may be old enough to collect Social Security, but how could you tell? Its stately, elegant appearance seems timeless. At 17 stories, the Delano was the tallest building in Miami Beach when completed in 1947, and its scale and style helped set a new tone for postwar development. No polychrome here! The crisp pleated bays of its pristine white façade give dimension to the window grid while allowing for the play of light and shadow. Its most distinctive exterior feature is the 4-finned tower that erupts at the roofline from the central section of the façade. The design may owe something to past streamlined motifs, but it remains entirely distinctive. Look for the name Delano discreetly embossed on the side of the tower. Inside is a different story: 30-foot tall billowing curtains in the lobby usher visitors into a dark wooded world created by designer Philippe Starck in the mid-1990s to suggest deluxe glamour and romance. Doors lead outside to an oceanside pool surrounded by manicured greenery that some consider the best on the beach. Romanian-born architect B. Robert Swartburg (1895–1975) enjoyed a thriving design practice in the greater Miami area but most consider the Delano Hotel his masterwork.

FONTAINEBLEAU HOTEL

4441 Collins Avenue
Morris Lapidus, 1954
North wing addition: A. Herbert Mathes, 1959
Renovation and expansions, Nichols, Brosch, Wurst, Wolfe & Associates, 1998, 2003

Morris Lapidus designed hundreds of projects during his long career (see M1-21, MB2-16) but the Fontainebleau Hotel really made him famous. His theatrical approach to design appealed to a prosperous post–World War II populace eager to enjoy a "staircase to nowhere" that encouraged women to make a grand entrance; glittering gigantic crystal chandeliers; a black and white bow-tie lobby floor suggesting gala tuxedo affairs; ceilings that seemed to float in the air; and curves everywhere, beginning with the 11-story crescent-shaped hotel itself. Built on the site of the 22-acre Firestone estate, the 554-room Fontainebleau Hotel developed by Ben Novack set a new Miami Beach standard as the largest and most glamorous hotel of its day. But drama ensued when Novak's former partner, Harry Mufson, hired Lapidus away to design the 14-story, 349-room Eden Roc Hotel next door. Rivalry continued when Novack retaliated by building the 15-story Versailles Tower so that it would keep Eden Roc's pool in shadow. Lapidus created pizzazz for the smaller hotel by interpreting the Italian Baroque theme in a Modernist way. Both hotels have recently undergone extensive renovations and major expansions designed by NBWW & Associates that add new towers and deluxe amenities.

HELEN MAR

2421 Pancoast Drive
Robert E. Collins, 1936

The 7-story Helen Mar, built on the west bank of Lake Pancoast, is a vivid landmark in this largely residential neighborhood. Its scale, style, and coloring give it a chic, head-turning kind of charm. Note its name boldly painted in fashionable Art Deco thick-and-thin letters on the roof block. As a freestanding structure, its chiseled sides, while not identical, are each finished faces that contribute to the overall composition. The concrete block building is surfaced in pale-toned stucco. The yellow-painted end bays have vertical ribbon windows outlined in blue that turn the corner. On the longer north and south façades, a 3-sided windowed bay in the same colors extends the full height of the building and three long horizontal lines of black glass mark the top story. The east and west exteriors have a salmon-colored band at the roofline that is repeated for the penthouse. Walls flanking the entry are embellished with six black glass stripes and a stylized bas-relief floral embedded panel. Now an 80-unit condominium, the Helen Mar was designed as an apartment hotel for contractor John Marsa. Architect Robert Elsmere Collins, in collaboration with Thomas Lamb, was also responsible for the Lincoln and Cameo theaters in Miami Beach.

MB2-7 2228 PARK AVENUE

Chad Oppenheim Architecture + Design, 2006

These two 4-story townhouses at 2228 Park Avenue were built as high-end infill housing in a mixed-use area. The site is an irregular trapezoidal lot at the intersection of several busy streets but within the Cultural Arts neighborhood that includes the Bass Museum of Art, the Miami City Ballet, and the Miami Beach Library. The back of the property faces the Collins Canal, with Dade Boulevard and the Miami Public Works Department beyond. Oppenheim envisioned both townhouses contained within a single rectangular volume, with parking and gardens on the ground floor, living quarters on the second and third levels, and two private pools on the roof. On the Park Avenue side, decorative perforated screening on the first two floors hides parking and can be backlit to add visual interest. The upper two floors are recessed and have long vertical windows, while the flat roof above provides sunshade. The rear side opens up with floor-to-ceiling windows across most of its surface, offering a contrast to the protected street façade. Unfortunately, in the midst of an economic downturn, the units remained empty. But the design was so appealing that the residential complex has recently been adapted for a new use: a nightclub.

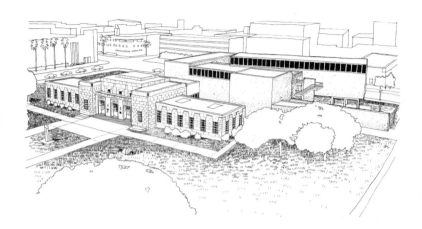

2100 Collins Avenue
Russell T. Pancoast, 1930
North and south additions: Russell T. Pancoast & Associates
Bass Museum conversion, Robert Swartburg, 1963
Addition and rehabilitation: Arata Isozaki with Spillis Candela DMJM, 2001
Originally John S. Collins Memorial Library

The Bass Museum of Art reveals the history and architecture of Miami Beach in several special ways: it sits on parkland donated to the city by John S. Collins, one of the three founders of Miami Beach; it was designed by his grandson, Russell Thorn Pancoast (1898–1972), as the John S. Collins Memorial Library; and it is a rare Miami Beach example of the classical Moderne style. The original 2-story, keystone-faced building is classically symmetrical but uses flattened ornament inspired by local, not ancient, forms. The building mass consists of a central recessed loggia set back in the horizontal plane and flanked by two taller blocks. In 1937 sculptor Gustav Bohland added three doorway friezes depicting Floridian motifs and fierce seagull gargoyles atop the sidewalls. Pancoast's sympathetic south (1937) and north (1950) wings create a long horizontal composition. The building became the Bass Museum of Art in 1963 after the library moved out, first to a new home built in front of it (demolished) and in 2005 to the nearby building designed by Robert Stern. In 2001 the Bass Museum entrance was rerouted when Arata Isozaki completed a stark rectangular addition on the west side. Fortunately the original building entrance and open park vistas have been reclaimed.

MB2-9 ALBION HOTEL

1650 James Avenue
Igor Polevitzky and Thomas Triplett Russell, 1939
Renovation: Studio Carlos Zapata, 1996

The Albion Hotel is a robust play on a nautical theme. It's 7-story height, ship railings, girth, repeated porthole windows at each level, and circular rooftop "smokestacks" all suggest ocean liner travel. Still, as a mixed-use complex with ground-floor retail and offices above on Lincoln Road and the hotel fronting James Avenue. it's much more about mass than decorative details. The Albion's entrance is a recessed rectangle that opens to a 2-story lobby. An interior courtyard—where peek-a-boo portholes provide glimpses of swimmers in the pool—connects the hotel's central section with wings for hotel amenities. The hotel was the work of two young architects who had met at the University of Pennsylvania, Igor Polevitzky (1911–1978) and Thomas Triplett Russell (1911–2000), and who were partners from 1935 until World War II intervened in 1941. Polevitzky, who would go on to design more than 500 buildings during his career, was an innovative, sophisticated architect with a European background whose later "inside-out" houses took advantage of the tropical South Florida climate. He is also known for designing the Havana Riviera Hotel. In 1996 the Albion Hotel was renovated by Carlos Zapata who created custom-designed furnishings and décor for a contemporary minimalist look.

1701 Washington Avenue
Albert Anis, Charles Raggio Greco, 1947
Addition: Morris Lapidus, 1967

Temple Emanu-El's majestic building dominates the busy intersection of 17th Street and Washington Avenue. The 10-story, 96,000-square-foot synagogue was built by the oldest Conservative congregation in Miami Beach at a cost of $1 million, an indication of the size and prosperity of its members who had once been part of the Orthodox Congregation of Beth Jacob (see MB1-3). The Temple Emanu-El complex includes a social hall on the north side facing Washington Avenue designed by Morris Lapidus. The original structure, designed by Albert Anis (1889–1964) and Charles R. Greco (1873–1962), features the octagonal Abraham Frost Sanctuary that seats 1,370 people with walls of arched windows and a dome above. The exterior reflects a kind of Spanish-Moorish influence with tall pylons flanking the entrance and reeded columns faced in pink-dyed keystone dividing the entrance doors. Above the doors and on either side of the entrance are intricate pierced-masonry screens. Anis, a member of the congregation, was a prolific local architect (see MB1-16, MB1-22). Greco, from Massachusetts, was an expert in designing churches and synagogues. He modeled Temple Emanu-El after similar rotunda-based temples he had previously designed, including Temple Beth Israel (1936) in Hartford, Connecticut, and especially Temple-Tifereth Israel (1924) in Cleveland, Ohio.

FILLMORE EAST MIAMI BEACH AT THE JACKIE GLEASON THEATER

1700 Washington Avenue
Pancoast & Associates, Henry Hohauser, L. Murray Dixon, 1948
Renovation: Morris Lapidus, 1974
Renovation: Jaime Borrelli and Markus Frankel and Peter Blitstein, 1988

The Jackie Gleason Theater of the Performing Arts has undergone many alterations since it opened in 1948. It was originally designed as the Miami Beach Auditorium by three of the best-known architects in the city. Its 3,500 seats were arranged arena style—indeed the auditorium was as well known for hosting boxing matches as for beauty pageants. Early views show an exterior composed of a three main elements: a long canopy over the driveway drop-off entrance with the words "Miami Beach Auditorium" displayed on top; a 2-story volume attached to it with nine vertical windows that provided light to the lobby; and, behind it, the taller rectangular mass of the auditorium itself. Jackie Gleason made the venue famous in the 1960s when he used it to broadcast his popular television show, and it was named in his honor after his death in 1987. Interior renovations, by Morris Lapidus in the 1970s and others, have been almost continuous for the past fifty years. In the late 1980s, Borrelli and Frankel and Blitstein, along with other work, modified the exterior to bring it more to the Art Deco appearance we see today. On the grounds, note Roy Lichtenstein's (1923–1977) *Mermaid*, the artist's first piece of public sculpture.

MB2-12 MIAMI BEACH CONVENTION CENTER

1901 Convention Center Drive
South Hall: B. Robert Swartburg, 1958
North Hall: Gilbert Fein, 1968
Wraparound meeting Rooms: Watson, Deutschman & Kruse, 1974
East Expansion: Jaime Borrelli and Markus Frankel and Peter Blitstein with Thompson, Ventulett, Stainbeck & Associates, 1987

The 1,000,000+-square-foot Miami Beach Convention Center began modestly in 1957 as the Miami Beach Exhibition Hall, a structure built to accommodate 15,000 people at once. Its site adjacent to the Miami Beach Auditorium, now the Jackie Gleason Theater of the Performing Arts (see MB2-11), helped create a public venue center. But to host large meetings such as the Republican Party convention in 1968, the facility had to expand. In 1968, Gilbert Fein (1919–2003) completed a large north addition. Born in Brooklyn, Fein received his architecture training at New York University and developed a flourishing practice in Florida after World War II, designing hundreds of residential and commercial buildings in the new Modern style. Twenty years later the collaborative design team of Borrelli and Frankel and Blitstein more than doubled the size of the convention center. They not only renovated the two older exhibition halls but also added a large section on the east side that includes two exhibit halls, 70 different-sized meeting rooms, 100,00 square feet of prefunction space, a continuous landscaped concourse that brings the outdoors in, and other essential service spaces and amenities. Note how the stepped concrete trellis and lantern on the Washington Avenue façade gestures to the historic Art Deco/Moderne neighborhood.

MIAMI BEACH
COMMUNITY CHURCH

500 Lincoln Road
Walter DeGarmo, 1921
Parish Hall
1620 Drexel Avenue
Russell T. Pancoast, 1949

Before Art Deco, Nautical, and Streamline movements came to Miami Beach, Mediterranean styles prevailed, as seen in this small white Spanish Revival church. The concrete building features cast-stone decorative door and rose window surrounds, referred to as Churrigueresque, that add dimensionality and interest to its otherwise plain face. Note also the pierced masonry roundels and simple arched doorways that flank the main entrance, the curved parapet, and the red barrel tile roof. Above the large rose window is an empty niche that seems waiting for a saint, although the church was initially Congregational and a bell was supposed to occupy the space. At his wife's insistence, so the story goes, developer Carl Fisher donated three valuable lots on Lincoln Road for a church. He hired the first registered architect in Florida to design it: Walter DeGarmo (1876–1952). DeGarmo had trained at Cornell University and worked with famed classicist John Russell Pope before moving to Coconut Grove in 1903. He was much in demand (see CG-9) during Miami's boom years, especially in upscale Coral Gables and Coconut Grove. But he changed with the times: his last project was a Modernist police precinct and courthouse for the City of Miami, now a landmark.

MIAMI BEACH CITY HALL

1700 Convention Center Drive
Grove Haack & Bouterse Borelli Albaisa, 1977
Floor mosaic: Carlos Alves, 2000
Renovation of ground-floor public areas: City of Miami Beach Property Management Division, 1996

Miami Beach City Hall Annex
Perkins & Will, 2010

Built some thirty years apart on the same city block, the Miami Beach City Hall and the new City Hall Annex offer a convenient comparison of two different approaches and programmatic requirements to municipal office design. Built in 1977, the 4-story unornamented concrete Miami Beach City Hall is a horizontal composition that spreads its long white arms along both Convention Center Drive and 17th Street, a distinct contrast to the verticality of the historic City Hall (see MB1-12). Raised on a berm, with parking underneath, it features an atrium at the northwest corner and a large floor plate on the top story that shades the floors below. The City Hall Annex is a 300,000-square-foot structure designed by Pat Bosch of Perkins & Will that includes 7 stories of parking and 4 floors totaling 35,000 square feet of municipal offices that line the west edge of the parking structure. Its glass and steel profile is crisp and metallic. A system of horizontal metal blades attached to but separated from the exterior of the parking garage gives this building its distinctive design. It connects to City Hall both by a thirrd-story pedestrian bridge walkway and a landscaped pedestrian plaza at the southwest corner of the site.

541 Lincoln Road
Gehry Partners, 2011
SoundScape Park: West 8

For Frank Gehry (b. 1930) the New World Symphony Center commission must have been appealing: a chance to tackle a favorite building type; to work with a trusted friend and client, New World Symphony founder and artistic director, Michael Tilson Thomas, for whom Gehry once babysat; and to complete his first building in Florida. The challenge? To connect orchestral music to the larger community while meeting the music academy's needs for classroom, office, rehearsal, parking, and performance space. From the outset, new technology was integrated into the design process in order to enhance the musical experience and to expand potential audiences. The 7-story structure, which faces a 2.5-acre public park dubbed "SoundScape," is a long rectangular box that consists of two parts: an 80-foot-high glass-walled atrium adjacent to a 736-seat performance space with a blank wall that serves as a 7,000-square-foot screen to project performances to outdoor viewers. A parking garage is to the rear. The atrium's interior contains boxy rooms jumbled on top of each other as well as curving stairs and narrow corridors that force interpersonal visibility. The performance space has nearly in-the-round seating and large adjustable curving panels on the stage for sound and projected video.

Between Washington Avenue and Alton Road
Carl Fisher, 1917; Additions: Morris Lapidus, 1957-61
Renovation: Thompson & Wood, 1995-96
400 Block: Studio Carlos Zapata

In 1915, when Miami Beach developer Carl Fisher carved through a dense mangrove thicket to create Lincoln Road, he envisioned the street as the heart of Miami Beach. Remarkably, it still is. In the early days the central six-block section (recently extended) of the street was lined with upscale retail shops and social gathering spots catering to the wealthy. But after World War II, Lincoln Road slumped as new developments further north, including the Fontainebleau Hotel and Bal Harbor, drew customers away. That's when Morris Lapidus (1902-2000) came to the rescue, determined to rid the road of cars. In 1957 he began working pro bono before being hired by the city. "Cars never bought anything," he pronounced. By 1961, his plans approved, Lincoln Road became a pedestrian promenade. But Lapidus did far more. He added "follies," concrete shapes using 20th-century technology that provide welcome shade and add interest to the strolling experience. He striped the pavement with diagonal white lines, added landscaping, and installed fountains and water pools. The Modernist update worked and was followed in the late 1990s with more trees and new follies designed by architects Carlos Zapata and Ben Wood. Don't miss the plaque at Euclid Avenue honoring Morris Lapidus.

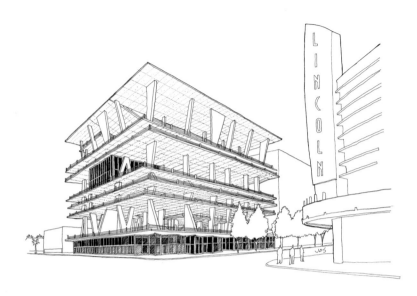

Herzog & de Meuron Architekten 2010

A parking garage rarely receives public acclaim. But 1111 Lincoln Road's sophisticated design defies conventional typology and makes possible the unexpected: civic engagement. The project required staged planning. First, the architects designed a new 4-story home for SunTrust Bank on Alton Road with residences on the top two floors; next they renovated the original 2-story Suntrust building on Lincoln Road to include ground-floor retail with offices above. The Lincoln Road pedestrian promenade was extended to Alton Road so that finally, the 243,000 square foot, 300-car concrete garage could be built on the prominent corner where the two roads meet. Although only 7 stories high, 1111 Lincoln Road has a monumental presence. It looms over its shorter neighbors and demands attention. The floor heights vary from 8 to 34 feet, conveying a sense of compression and release, as do the trapezoidal columns that support the floors. There are no walls above the ground floor retail shops, and cables marking the upper floor edges are nearly invisible. Finally the garage includes a center staircase, a retail shop in the midst of the fifth floor, and a rooftop penthouse and restaurant. Unobstructed spans and panoramic views offer dramatic space for public or private events. Parking is convenient.

PUBLIX ON THE BAY

1920 West Avenue
Wood & Zapata, 1998

In Miami Beach, grocery shopping can be a design experience if your destination is the Publix on West Avenue. Locals call it the "Mothership," "Guggenheim," or "Jetsons" Publix, depending on their frame of reference. Designed by Venezuelan-born-architect-dubbed-Modernist-maverick Carlos Zapata (see MB2-9, MB-16), the structure explores the theatrical aspects of a humdrum task and property type by reimagining the grocery store trip as a personal journey. Two levels of parking are placed above a standard 50,000-square-foot Publix store. They are contained in a striking steel and glass aerodynamic mass positioned at an upward angle that suggests a modern ocean liner ready to embark on some celestial adventure. The parking is attached to the store via a 3-story glass hall connected to the street and storefront where highly visible customers with shopping carts on steep moving ramps animate the structure. Elevators and scissors stairs offer additional circulation options. The 1.92-acre site, formerly owned by Florida Power & Light, was targeted by the City of Miami Beach for a new grocery store. Although this store is unique, Publix Super Markets, like Apple and Target, uses good design as part of its branding mission. That focus has clearly brought public attention and shoppers here.

Monument Island
Sculptors: H. P. Peterson, Ettore Pellegatta, 1920
Restoration: STA Architectural Group, 2009

The Flagler Memorial was built for a visionary, Henry Morrison Flagler, by another visionary, Carl G. Fisher. They never met, but Fisher (1874–1939) admired Flagler (1830–1913), whose Florida East Coast Railroad created so many opportunities for real estate development in the state. Fisher first came to Miami Beach in 1912 after he had made his fortune in the automotive parts business and began developing the area as a resort for the wealthy. The 96-foot-tall Flagler monument is fashioned after the Washington Monument, the most famous obelisk in the country. Sculptors H. P. Peterson and Ettore Pellegatta (1881–1966) both worked on the project. On the base are four allegorical figures corresponding to the compass points: Prosperity, Pioneer, Education, and Industry. At a time when new islands were being created for real estate developments, Fisher had a perfect circular island made with the Flagler Memorial as the centerpiece. He later donated it to the City of Miami Beach as a public park. Natural forces and man-made damage have wreaked havoc on the Flagler Memorial. The island, which never had a protective sea wall built around it, is irregularly shaped now and overgrown, though the city and volunteers do some maintenance. The Flagler monument however, was recently restored.

INDEX OF ARCHITECTS

INDEX OF BUILDINGS

(*Italics* indicate buildings referenced in text.)